Earthquake Exodus, 1906

Looking out from the flatlands of Berkeley toward the flames and huge smoke clouds that rose above San Francisco.

EARTHQUAKE EXODUS, 1906

Berkeley Responds to the San Francisco Refugees

RICHARD SCHWARTZ

RSB BOOKS
BERKELEY, CALIFORNIA

RSB Books
telephone and fax: 510-524-1683
email: AMRSB@worldnet.att.net

Editor: Judith Dunham
Copyeditor: Pamela Joy Edelstein
Design: Lisa Elliot/Elysium

Cover photo reproduced from *The San Francisco Catastrophe.*

ISBN: 0-9678204-1-3

First printing, 2005
Printed in the United States of America

10 9 8 7 6 5 4 3 2 1

Contents

A lone live oak on the Palache estate (located just northwest of the future site of the Claremont Hotel) before development of the land into an upscale residential neighborhood.

FOREWORD

Though it ruptured more than three hundred miles of the San Andreas Fault, the mighty earthquake of April 18, 1906, will forever be known for the city it only indirectly destroyed: San Francisco. Other Northern California towns were jostled as violently—a few seconds of furious shaking flattened downtown Santa Rosa and much of Stanford University, for example. But by felling San Francisco's chimneys and rupturing its water mains, the earthquake provided ideal conditions for a conflagration that swept away what Robert Louis Stevenson once ominously dubbed "a woodyard of unusual extent and complication," temporarily erasing one of the nation's greatest cities and rendering a quarter-million people homeless. For three days and nights, people in the East Bay watched the metropolis burn and listened to the concussions of dynamite drift across the water.

Prima donna that she is, San Francisco has always upstaged those other cities that her own citizens regard as mere bit players and supporting actors in the Bay Area. In the tragedy of 1906, she had a starring role to which—not surprisingly—Sarah Bernhardt likened her own performance of *Phèdre* a month later in UC Berkeley's Greek Theatre. After a century, however, Richard Schwartz reminds us that the earthquake left a lasting imprint on other cities as well.

On April 17, 1906, the university town had twenty-six thousand residents. A year later, it had grown by half again to thirty-eight thousand, largely due to the influx of homeless refugees fleeing the afflicted city. Schwartz explains how Berkeleyans generously responded by setting up temporary camps, dispensing food, listing jobs, and even taking in the homeless. He details the measures taken to ensure public order and health as city and university officials struggled to deal with thousands of disoriented, impoverished, and sometimes dangerous strangers, many separated from their loved ones—everyday details long forgotten but worth study by those who wish to better prepare for the next great shake.

San Francisco's misfortune was a godsend for East Bay real estate agents and developers, for ex-urban refugees quickly discovered they could buy suburban lots far cheaper and with more benign weather than those of the fog-shrouded city by the Golden Gate. The recent advent of electricity and telephones, as well as excellent train service provided by the Key Route and Southern Pacific systems, increased the value of properties throughout the region and encouraged subdivision of the last farms in Berkeley. In the Mason-McDuffie Company, Berkeley fortunately had one of the most enlightened developers in the country. That the quake happened at the height of the Arts and Crafts movement —and that UC Berkeley had just established the West's first College of Architecture—produced a bumper crop of fascinating houses, churches, and clubhouses that literally distinguish the town to this day. Schwartz reminds us that today's Berkeley, as much as San Francisco, is largely the result of that shaking a century ago.

— Dr. Gray Brechin, geographer and author of
Imperial San Francisco: Urban Power, Earthly Ruin
Berkeley, California

INTRODUCTION

The earthquake that struck at 5:14 a.m. on April 18, 1906, was felt from Coos Bay, Oregon, to Los Angeles and into eastern Nevada. Destruction was unleashed unevenly throughout California from Fresno to Eureka within thirty miles on either side of the newly named San Andreas Fault. People all around the San Francisco Bay felt the quake, but their experiences were remarkably different. Some sensed only mild shaking; others witnessed complete devastation. For tens of thousands, it would be the last time they awoke in their own beds in their own homes.

To date, no book has told the story of the city of Berkeley's experience during and after the earthquake, or of its response to the thousands of refugees who poured into Berkeley seeking relief from the ravages thrust upon San Francisco by the quake and subsequent fire.

Compared with the earthquake's impact in San Francisco, Berkeley was only moderately rattled. Almost every chimney was knocked down. Many buildings were damaged, and a few were destroyed. Collapsed chimneys, dislodged electrical wires, and flammable substances thrown from shelves ignited fires, but Berkeley firefighters, working efficiently with a plentiful water supply, were able to squelch the flames before they could spread from building to building and engulf sections of town. In the absence of functioning power and telegraph lines (two-way phones were not a reality yet in Berkeley), Berkeley residents had to ask their neighbors for news of the extent of the disaster. Most stood outside their homes quietly talking about what had occurred and wondering how bad the situation was elsewhere. As they looked west, however, they could see huge, broad plumes of black smoke rising above sections of San Francisco forming massive black clouds slowly drifting toward them on a gentle morning breeze.

This sudden firestorm, not the damage from the earthquake, was what ultimately destroyed so much of the city. Along with the spreading flames and choking smoke, San Franciscans were assaulted by dust from collapsed buildings, the sight of dead bodies, and the nearly overwhelming chaos and panic.

When word spread that Berkeley and other East Bay towns were safe havens, they fled to ferry terminals and train stations, seeking a way across the bay.

Within hours of the quake, before the San Francisco refugees arrived in numbers, Berkeley residents came together and began to prepare for what would be an unprecedented wave of stricken, exhausted refugees. Berkeley's relief assistance was notable for a number of reasons. It was conceived and run by ordinary citizen volunteers who did not wait for the government to take the initiative. Their efforts were extraordinarily well-organized and took advantage of scientific and military principles and procedures that figured into the backgrounds of many Berkeley residents. The entire town—individuals, businesses, fraternal and religious organizations, and the university—mobilized in a concerted way and opened their homes and wallets, along with their hearts, to the refugees.

The relief effort lasted only about ten weeks. By the time it was over, refugees had established themselves as new Berkeley residents, found homes or employment elsewhere, or returned to San Francisco. Despite the brevity of the relief period, it had a lasting impact on both Berkeley and San Francisco. The story of both the refugees who fled to Berkeley and the Berkeleyans who met them with open arms has been neglected by history. *Earthquake Exodus, 1906* tells their story, accompanied by many photographs, a number of them published for the first time. My hope is that this book not only offers insight about Berkeley's and San Francisco refugees' experience of the 1906 earthquake, but also inspires us to react to future tragedies with the same compassion and determination displayed by citizens a century ago.

— Richard Schwartz

Looking north on Shattuck Avenue from Addison Street, circa 1903.

Chapter One
APRIL 17, BERKELEY

*H*arold Yost had trained himself to wake up a couple of minutes before his alarm clock rang at 5:15 a.m. As he bounded out of bed that Tuesday morning, the thirteen-year-old paperboy noticed that the fog had not come in during the night. It would be another nice day.

With his newspaper bag slung over his shoulder, he walked briskly from his house at 2201 Hearst Avenue, at the northeast corner of Hearst and Oxford Street, to the spot where he counted out the papers for his route. On the way he passed lath, bags of plaster, and framing lumber stacked up on the streets where houses were being built. At Shattuck Avenue, just south of University Avenue, dependable Mr. Hill was right on time. His horse-drawn two-wheel wagon was filled with bundles of the *San Francisco Chronicle,* which he had picked up earlier at the ferry wharf near Jack London Square. Hill always let the boys unload the papers from his wagon. Harold paused to look at the headlines in the fresh edition, dated April 17, 1906.[1]

As Harold worked his route up Hearst to Euclid Avenue and then turned north, he was accustomed to seeing construction workers hustle materials around their work sites. He would listen carefully to their banter, trying to catch a new curse word or phrase he could use to impress his friends at recess.

Construction workers were a common sight ever since the building boom began in 1903. That year service had started on the San Francisco, Oakland & San Jose Railway electric trains, commonly known as the Key Route. Clusters of new residences were going up near the tracks, many of them occupied by people who preferred Berkeley's mild weather to the colder climate of San Francisco,

Bill the Hot Dog Man operated a stand on the east side of Shattuck Avenue by Center Street. Local students came by for lunch and to enjoy Bill's jokes and sleights of hand. Berkeleyans of all ages showed up to hear him sing as he rhythmically chopped food on his cutting board. The sign on his stand read "Eat here, die at home."

The Key Route Pier south of Berkeley was the hub of the
system of trains and ferries operated by the San Francisco,
Oakland & San Jose Railway. The opulent terminal with
its ferry slips resembled a key with notches. It was built in
1903 and destroyed by a fire thirty years later.

Passengers walking from the ferry slips to their connecting
trains at the Key Route Pier.

along with the more affordable prices. A quick, smooth, and quiet ride on the electrically lit modern train brought the commuters to the railway's connecting ferry line at the terminal, or mole, about three miles south of the Berkeley Pier. The entire trip from downtown Berkeley to San Francisco took only thirty-six minutes.

According to the word around town, a new two-story brick building would be erected at Shattuck Avenue and Center Street in Berkeley's thriving downtown. A block south, a "for sale" sign hung at 2169 Shattuck Avenue. The $3,000 asking price marked the recent rise in real estate prices.

Other than the sounds of construction, it had been rather quiet of late, except for the death of well-known businessman Otto Niehaus. The fifty-nine-year-old co-owner of the West Berkeley Planing Mill had died at his home on 1729 Ninth Street the night before. His brother Edward, with partner Schuster, bought the two-year-old mill in 1876, and Otto, an engineer and machinist, had joined the successful firm as a supervisor four years later. With business booming, he

The West Berkeley Planing Mill, one of the biggest on the West Coast, was started in 1874 and bought by Schuster and Edward Niehaus in 1876. After several expansions, it occupied an area of 105 x 100 feet, containing 20,000 square feet of space. The mill made doors and windows and their frames, as well as moldings, mantels, cabinets, fencing, tanks, windmills, stepladders, and decorative trim.

Employment for Chinese men was limited to certain trades. Many established Berkeley families with financial means employed Chinese houseboys for decades and often related to them as members of the family.

picked a bad time to leave.

Later that day, the Berkeley Chamber of Commerce intended to discuss the need for a new wharf at the foot of University Avenue. Many in town wanted deep-water facilities that could accommodate large ships, hoping that this improvement would lead to filling the waterfront area with industry.

The economic growth and prospect of work had attracted many single men and women to Berkeley. They typically lodged in same-sex boardinghouses. As jobs were plentiful, rentals abounded to meet the demand. On April 17, a newcomer could rent "sunny furnished rooms" at 2515 Regent Street, a two-story shingle house nestled off the street, for $17.50 to $22.50 per month. Asian workers found employment through agencies like Mitonta's Japanese and Chinese Employment Office at 2028 Center Street. The real estate boom was also good for Harold Yost and his fellow paperboys. Want ad space was growing along with subscriptions.

The area bordered by San Pablo Avenue on the west and Milvia Street on the east was still mostly farmland, though developers were methodically acquiring tracts. The hardy pioneer farmers were now old men and ready to sell their properties. Boys complained about losing their secret spots as houses sprung up where they had always chased jackrabbits through open fields and hid among clusters of trees to smoke cigarettes.

North of Eunice Street, Berkeley's northern boundary, were the ranchlands.

Looking eastward from the ranchlands beyond the 1906 boundaries of Berkeley. After the earthquake, this area would become the neighborhood of Northbrae.

Looking east up Eunice Street, the northern boundary of the city of Berkeley in the early twentieth century.

ABOVE: *The UC cadets performed drills in what was most likely the old baseball field on campus, located where the Life Sciences Building stands today.*

RIGHT: *The UC cadets in formation in front of North Hall with their band and admirers on hand.*

To townsfolk, the area seemed far away, even remote, especially since the only way to reach the area was on a few dirt paths. Areas like the Elmwood, southeast of downtown and not served by the Key Route trains, also seemed distant. Travel in general was neither easy nor fast. In good weather the dirt roads were dusty; in bad, muddy and rutted. Cars were very rare, and horses were only for those who could afford them. For most people, travel was limited to public transportation and the constraints of a ten- to twelve-hour workday, six days a week. Taking the train to Idora Park on Telegraph Avenue or Shellmound Park in Emeryville for a Sunday picnic was a big social event.

At the University of California campus, the UC cadets' ROTC (Reserve Officer Training Corps) department had a day to prepare for its annual inspection drills, due to begin at sunrise the next morning. Because the university was a federally funded land grant college, an officer-training program had been part of the school since its inception. Once a year, the army generals came to Berkeley to check out their investment. Captain Nance, one of the cadets' commanders, pushed his troops especially hard that day, making sure they would be ready for the April 18 review.

By the end of the workday, the construction sites grew quiet and the commuters returned home by ferry and train. Many residents preferred a relaxing evening at home following a walk to the neighborhood corner store to buy a bottle of their favorite beer and a newspaper to be read by a kerosene light before going to sleep. The agile and energetic headed out for an evening of roller-skating at 2038 Center Street, one of Berkeley's rinks. Women were always admitted free, and Merritt's Military Band played from 7:30 to 10:30 p.m. The more sedate attended L. W. Rogers's lecture, "Reincarnation: What It Is and What It Is Not," at Woodmen Hall at 2180 Center Street. A handful of audience members had already bought tickets for his lecture the following night, "Karma: Nature's Law of Justice."

City employees enjoyed a celebratory dinner at Emile Bruel's trendy saloon and French restaurant, the Poplar Villa Café, at 2224 Fourth Street in West Berkeley. When it was city attorney Redmond "Ready" Staats's turn to speak, he was introduced as "Steady Rats." The crowd went into hysterics and throughout the evening continued to replay the gaffe. Everyone started home well after midnight, laughing their way into the early morning of April 18.

City employee Redmond Staats.

APRIL 17 IN GALVESTON, TEXAS

Telegraph operator E. M. Thurston knew something was wrong. As he dozed off that Tuesday night, he was awakened by the sputtering of his telegraph equipment. Initially, Thurston thought someone in the Gulf of Mexico area was attempting to reach his station. He tried to answer, but no one responded. As the night progressed, the signals got more erratic, and Thurston began to think that the wires were "possessed." He meticulously inspected everything in the station for malfunctions. Having found none, he signaled Denver and east St. Louis to see if operators there were trying to contact him, which might have accounted for the behavior of his equipment. They had not. Thurston's equipment became so charged that shortly after midnight he was forced to stop using his telegraph keys.

On Wednesday morning, after Thurston learned of the San Francisco earthquake, he was convinced that it had affected the air currents, which, in turn, subtly but profoundly impacted the telegraph wires and his wireless station equipment. Deciding to remain on duty, he recorded identical reactions in his telegraph equipment when new quakes and aftershocks struck, including a temblor felt in Los Angeles. He noticed that the disturbances to the wires and equipment started hours before each quake. Thurston came to the conclusion that his sensitive equipment could anticipate seismic activity. Scientists began studying Thurston's theories in the hopes of finding a practical application.

This photograph, offering a view of San Francisco's Market Street from the corner of Mason and Eddy streets, was taken within fifteen minutes of the earthquake. All of the buildings were later destroyed by the fires that swept the area.

Chapter Two
APRIL 18, 5:14 A.M.

Before Harold Yost had gone to bed, his mother, Julia, made sure he finished his school report on the April 7 eruption of Mt. Vesuvius. She saw that he was asleep early so he could get up in time to start his paper route. Just as Harold awoke, a violent shaking erupted, almost knocking him from his bed. His mother rushed into his room. "It's an earthquake," she said, "and I don't know what's going to happen to us. You'd better get up right away."[1]

At the same moment, Phil Teague, son of Berkeley pioneer William Teague, was aroused by the shaking of his home at 2203 McKinley Avenue. The plumber and former Berkeley volunteer fireman ran to the back porch. Holding the rail to steady himself, he continued to feel the earth's undulations. He looked up after studying the ground and was mesmerized as a broom, which had been leaning on its bristles against the garage, danced across the yard. Policeman Wooley was on graveyard duty at the Berkeley Station at Shattuck and Center. "It seemed to me as though the streets were rising up," he later recalled. "It seemed as though the oscillation of the buildings was several feet. I could hardly keep [on] my feet."[2]

Wanting to occupy himself and thinking it best to get away from his nervous mother, Harold decided to pick up the papers for his route. He waited for his boss, Mr. Hill, at the usual spot, but everything felt different. Yost later reminisced, "On that particular morning, Hilly, as we kids called him, was later than usual, and as he drove up he was not smiling. One of the kids said, 'What's the matter Hilly? Did the earthquake hit you?' Hilly shook his head. 'I didn't feel any earthquake in my cart, but as I came along I wondered why so many people

Phil Teague with his wife, Elizabeth, and daughter, Cora. His father, William, was a pioneer of Berkeley. The Teague family still resides in Phil's home.

The Poet, His Animals, and the Earthquake

Poet Joaquin Miller was an early riser, so it was not surprising he was lying awake in bed a little after 5 a.m. on April 18, listening to the dawn chorus of birds. He then heard the cattle on his seventy-acre Oakland hills estate begin to moan far earlier than usual. Next his cats ran under his brass bed. He thought they were hiding from a stray dog. "I never witnessed such stillness," he wrote. The stillness was "terrible" and the light "unnatural."

Miller suddenly felt a slight jolt, as if he was "in a small boat bumping against a wharf." He wondered if the cause was an earthquake and went to his doorway. His Japanese laborers came by, and everyone confirmed each others' suspicions. Miller shuffled back to bed and the cats scampered out from their hiding place. After rising and having breakfast, Miller began working in his garden and noticed smoke "curling up . . . high and strong" in San Francisco.

Animals all over the Bay Area were harbingers of the earthquake. Dogs were heard howling the night of April 17. Some were seen running, their tails between their legs. After the quake, both dogs and cats ran away for days. Females took their young to safer quarters.

The night before the earthquake, horses were unusually restless and kicked at their stalls. A number of fire department horses became agitated and broke from their stalls. In a stable on Alhambra Street in San Francisco, a stableman had just fed his thirty horses. Twenty-five of them broke their halters and surrounded him. He was forced to keep them at bay with a pitchfork.

Wild animals confined in zoos quietly crouched down when the quake struck, but made a lot of noise when it was over. The elephant at The Chutes amusement park in San Francisco roared loudly not only after the quake but also following every aftershock.

Oakland poet Joaquin Miller posing on his land in front of the cottage he named "The Abby." He called the land "The Hights," an intentional misspelling. The cottage is still standing, in a park bearing his name on Joaquin Miller Road in Oakland.

were out on the streets so early, so I stopped at Alcatraz Avenue to find out. They told me there had been a pretty hard earthquake, but that was all they knew. It worries me, somehow.'"[3]

No one yet knew the true extent of the damage. In the absence of radios or telephones, news traveled by word of mouth, newspapers, and telegraph wires. Despite a big push to instigate telephone service in Berkeley, only 691 of the fifty-cents-per-month "kitchen phones" had been installed by 1900. Even so, these were only one-way ringerless phones used by housewives to order the delivery of supplies. The service did not allow calls to be received.

Reports of injuries spread as stunned residents gathered to talk about what they had just experienced. When the earthquake hit, Obe Decker, a downtown businessman, jumped from his bed. In his confused and panicked state, he fled his bedroom, but tripped at the top of the stairs, tumbled to the bottom, and badly sprained his right leg. W. J. Phillips of 1924 Channing Way had a similar mishap. Awakened by the quake, he instinctively grabbed his young daughter. Rushing down the stairs, he stumbled and sprained his ankle. Train brakeman C. A. Renfrow, who lived in a boardinghouse at 623 Bristol Street (now the west end of Hearst), bolted from his bed and went out the window. It was not known if he jumped or was thrown out by the earthquake.

One person was confirmed to have jumped out a window. Gustave Wagner, who resided at 1928 Channing Way, rented a room to Mrs. Hollenbeck. When the shaking began, she thought that the walls of the house were collapsing and believed she had to jump out the window to save her life. When doctors arrived, they found she had a severely strained back and feared she might have sustained internal injuries.

There were many stories of near escapes. UC philosophy professor George Howison and his family lived in a beautiful home at 2731 Bancroft Way. The previous evening had been warm, so the kids wanted to sleep out on the porch, as the family, and many other Berkeleyans, often did. Howison and his family were startled when the brick chimney crashed down around them as the earthquake began. The masonry contractor had used beach sand to mix up his mortar, and the bricks could not hold together during the twenty-eight seconds of shaking. Although the roar of the toppling bricks was deafening, the family felt

Portrait of UC philosophy professor George Howison. The chimney on his home tumbled down during the earthquake, but his family was unharmed.

lucky to be unharmed.

The most striking account of a chimney collapse involved the Meekers' two-week-old infant who was buried in its crib by the brick rubble of a collapsed fireplace. Most of the chimneys that collapsed were on the exterior of houses. Interior chimneys seemed to hold up better due to the support of floor and ceiling framing members. The April 26 *Berkeley Gazette* reported that "not a chimney was left standing from Hayward to Martinez." Five thousand were damaged or destroyed in Berkeley alone.

Andrew Donough was luckier than the Meekers. Donough, a well-known dry goods merchant on Shattuck Avenue, was up early, sitting at his kitchen table and going over his orders for the day. He had lit a kerosene lamp and set it near where he was working, next to an open window. At the onset of the earthquake, his house groaned and jolted. The horizontal motion threw the lamp into the air and onto the floor, where it tipped over and spilled its fuel, which burst into flames. Donough jumped up, seized the lamp, and threw it out the open window. He then grabbed a broom and a towel and chased the flames around the room until he extinguished them. Out of breath, he looked up to see his family staring at him, wide-eyed and disheveled.

The shaking at Berkeley architect George Ploughman's house was so loud that the family did not hear the bricks from the chimney crashing onto the roof. When the cacophony stopped, the family went outside and saw neighbors in all manner of bedclothes standing in their backyards. The family went inside and had breakfast. When asked what he had thought when woken by the earthquake, Ploughman's son said he believed a "big robber was trying to shake the house down so that he could [get] in."[4]

The chimney at 2461 Warring Street (left) collapsed along with many others in Berkeley. Ironically, this was the home of UC professor Andrew C. Lawson (above), who had just identified and named the San Andreas Fault.

BERKELEY'S DYNAMITERS

Broken water mains frustrated the firemen battling the fires that engulfed San Francisco after the earthquake. In a desperate attempt to create firebreaks and thwart the fast-moving flames, firemen, policemen, and military men dynamited buildings, leveling three structures at a time. Unfortunately, the explosions sent embers high into the air, only to fall and begin new fires. The sounds of exploding dynamite could be heard across the bay.

Some of the dynamite came from the California Powder Works, whose business office was in Berkeley. One of the company's plants was about a mile and a half north of town. John Bermingham Jr., the company's superintendent, was in charge of the demolition operations on the morning of April 18.

On April 27, after the fires had subsided, the powder works office at 2171 Shattuck Avenue, in the Berkeley Gazette Building, sent a bill of $4,000 to San Francisco Mayor Eugene E. Schmitz. The mayor reviewed the bill and thought it was reasonable, so he approved payment. A day later, the mayor received the same bill in the mail, but it was stamped "PAID IN FULL." An accompanying letter asked the mayor to consider the value of the bill as a donation from the company to the city in its hours of need.

The Phelan Building, at Market and O'Farrell streets, was dynamited in an effort to create a firebreak. The building housed the headquarters of the US Department of the Army. The army evacuated at 11 a.m. on April 18. The Chronicle Building is on the right, with a tower at its apex.

Chapter Three
VIEWING THE DAMAGE

Despite the earthquake, Harold Yost decided to deliver his papers. As he started his route around 6:30 a.m., Berkeley seemed about the same as always, except that people were outside their houses, milling around and talking. They were unaware of the damage beyond their neighborhood, yet deep down were worried.

Panorama of the Contra Costa Water Company reservoir in North Berkeley, circa 1906.

Harold passed his own house and saw his mother out on the porch. "I guess the house is all right," she yelled to him, "but I'm going to stay out here for a while." She promised him breakfast when he was done with his route. He continued up the hill to Le Conte Avenue. There he saw "the first of the great quake's calling cards: bricks that had once been outside chimneys scattered across a front lawn, with people clustered around looking dazed and worried, chatting in subdued tones."[1] As he went up Euclid, he was sobered to discover much more of the same.

From this point, he had a view across the bay. He was taken aback by what he saw—a growing cloud of black smoke rising over the city of San Francisco.

He didn't connect the smoke with the earthquake and scurried home for breakfast. Afterward, he changed into his school clothes, picked up his report on Mt. Vesuvius, stuffed it into his bag, and headed to school. He was unaware that the water main from the nearby North Berkeley reservoir had broken, sending a huge geyser of water into the air. Many people living along his paper route had fled to the hills.

School didn't start until 9 a.m., but Harold always went earlier to play games in the schoolyard. By 8:30 he was on his way up Oxford Street, not far from his house, when he spotted a schoolmate running toward him, waving his

Berkeley High School immediately after the earthquake. The school remained closed until repairs, estimated at $10,000, were made.

At the top of Dwight Way, nestled at the base of the Berkeley hills, was the School for the Deaf and Blind. The earthquake dislodged all of the chimneys. The girls' dormitory, Durham Hall, needed extensive repairs. The north turret of Moss Hall was cracked, and school officials feared it could easily topple in an aftershock. The main building's roof was racked to the north by four inches. Its massive clock had stopped at 5:14 a.m. In spite of this, classes were held as usual, but outside on the school grounds.

arms and yelling, "No school! They have got to see if the building's safe before we go back," Harold's friend told him. "But they say somethin's happened to Berkeley High. Let's go down and see."

The high school at Allston Way and Grove Street (now Martin Luther King Jr. Way) was Berkeley's pride and joy. Built five years earlier at a cost of $87,000, it was an impressive, two-story brick structure, with two tall brick chimneys rising above the handsome slate roof. Harold and his buddy ran down Milvia Street, then stopped abruptly when they saw that the chimneys were gone. In their place were two great gaping holes. Two matching piles of brick rubble lay on the ground directly below them. "Plaster was broken from the walls of near-ly every room," the evening *Oakland Tribune* of April 18 reported, "and the great flues in the attic were torn down by falling bricks."[2] A huge structural crack marred the northwest wing. The boys were stunned.

As it turned out, Berkeley schools—including Whittier, McKinley, Hillside, and San Pablo—suffered disproportionately to other buildings in the city. Hazel Skaggs, a student at the time, remembered, "Our brand new Washington School [Grove Street and Bancroft Way], a red brick building, toppled that morning. It had been completed only the day before."[3]

The buildings on the University of California campus fared much better.

In the northern end of Berkeley, word spread that the town's most magnificent and elegant edifice—St. Joseph's Academy, a private boys' school at the end of Albina Avenue off Hopkins Street—was "badly twisted." Some people reported being grazed by falling bricks.

When the damages were finally assessed, the estimate for all repairs was about $200. North Hall, one of the university's two original buildings, had been marked for demolition before the quake, but survived without a hint of damage. Among the biggest rumors in town was that the magnificent Greek Theatre had been split in two. People flocked to see it, only to find it intact. Some residents sought out the theater as a refuge from aftershocks. Architect John Galen Howard's California Hall had just been completed in August of 1905 and remained untouched by the quake. Elsewhere on campus, chimneys were dislodged from buildings, books were toppled from library shelves, and fragile chemistry equipment was thrown to the floor and shattered.

The university's more significant losses were in San Francisco, where a number of its buildings were destroyed. Its Mark Hopkins Institute of Art and most of the world-renowned artworks inside burned in the fires that followed the earthquake. A valuable law library, about to be shipped to its new home on the Berkeley campus, was also lost to the fire. Destruction of the university's

ABOVE: *The Standard Soap Works, a four-story wooden building dating from 1874, covered the entire block between Addison Street and Allston Way and Second and Third streets. The cost of repairing the earthquake-damaged chimney was estimated at $500–$600.*

LEFT: *Stiles Hall on the UC campus, badly damaged in the earthquake, survived and played a central role in the earthquake relief effort.*

income property on Market Street and the decline in real estate value of its other San Francisco holdings delayed completion of the Doe Library, then under construction on the Berkeley campus.

Official accounts of the earthquake's impact on the Berkeley campus did not include Stiles Hall on the southwest corner of Allston and Dana, which was a student center, primarily for YMCA and YWCA activities, and supported by private funds. After years of hard use, the 1892 hall had undergone many needed repairs in the summer of 1905, which, a July 1906 report noted, "were utterly ruined by the earthquake." The chimneys fell, and the roof was punctured with large holes. The rain that arrived a week later destroyed the plaster. The trustees' estimate for restoration and improvements totaled $1,200.

Chimneys and other tall, heavy structures throughout Berkeley were particularly vulnerable. The huge brick stack at the four-story Standard Soap Works, the largest soap factory west of the Mississippi, shifted off its base. Concerned that the chimney might collapse, manager Mark Sherwin sent home some of his crew. The chimney at the nearby O'Neil Glass Factory—an unusual conical form about fifty feet tall and seventy-five feet wide at its base—was

ABOVE: *The Southern Pacific Railroad ran both passenger and freight trains within and through Berkeley. This train, at the University Avenue Station, was known as the Overland Limited. The tall water tower was a probable duplicate of the one that crashed down on San Pablo Avenue and Carlton Street during the earthquake.*

RIGHT: *Henry Bruns moved to West Berkeley in 1874. Four years later he built this general store, which became one of the focal points of the early Oceanview district. He and his wife, along with their nine children, lived in the eighteen rooms above the store. The building was damaged in the earthquake.*

damaged as well. A hundred-foot-tall water tower at San Pablo Avenue and Carlton Street in Oceanview tipped over just as the morning's first train came down the San Pablo tracks. The train's crew worked for more than an hour to clear the debris from the tracks.

Police officer W. H. McCoy, working his beat in the Oceanview, was standing at San Pablo and University avenues when the earthquake struck. The stone walls of the elegant West Berkeley Bank on the northwest corner shattered, the building shifted off its foundation, and the masonry cornices fell to the ground. One section weighing thousands of pounds flew past McCoy's face and crashed at his feet. Dust blanketed his cup of coffee as he stood frozen and stunned. The bank, whose president was Berkeley's acting mayor Francis Ferrier, had been a symbol of the financial importance of Oceanview. At the same time McCoy saw the walls of the D. H. Bruns General Merchandising store across the street buckle. His attention was suddenly drawn to an explosion at the El Dorado Oil Works laboratory, at the northwest corner of University Avenue and Second Street. McCoy rushed to the nearest fire alarm box and then promptly pulled

the alarm on a second box. Firemen from two stations arrived and extinguished the oil works fire, which could have quickly engulfed the entire west end of town. Sadly for the workingmen of Oceanview, Charles Hadlen's and Dennis Landregren's saloons, popular watering holes, displayed significant damage. Several blocks away, a large crack in the roadbed of University Avenue ran west all the way until the street ended.

Downtown Berkeley, centered at Shattuck Avenue and Dwight Way, was especially hard-hit. The Barker Block building, on the northwest corner, had just been completed, and its owner, J. L. Barker, was about to place advertisements seeking tenants. The masonry cornice, shaken loose by the earthquake, lay shattered on the sidewalk. The building's awning hung limply. Damage to the interior was particularly extensive. "The building still stands," the April 18 *Oakland Tribune* reported, "but the upper story is little more than a pile of bricks. It is simply rent through and through." Across the street on the northeast corner, all the structures behind the Foy Block building were destroyed, and their collapse crushed other sheds attached to the rear of the building. The owner feared that the cost of repairs would reach $5,000.

An *Oakland Tribune* reporter wrote in the April 18 paper that downtown Berkeley was an "indescribable scene of confusion." At stores and pharmacies

About ten minutes after the quake, what was described as a wall of water five feet tall slammed into this West Berkeley Lumber Company wharf, destroying more than a hundred feet of the wharf and washing away an estimated fifty thousand feet of lumber. An employee, B. J. Rose, was securing a stack of lumber to a piling when the wave hit. He was thrown into the bay but was able to climb to safety. The tall chimney stack on the far right, part of the 1876 O'Neil Glass Factory, was also damaged in the earthquake.

such as Rolla Fuller's on Dwight and Bowman's on Center, merchants stood knee-deep in glass containers shattered on the floor and merchandise thrown off shelves. Downed electrical wires ignited a fire at Pond's Pharmacy on Shattuck near Center. The proprietor of Sorenson's crockery shop on Center arrived to find the store filled with the shards of once-expensive merchandise, and cracks opened up in the walls of the Carnegie Library at the southwest corner of Shattuck and Kittredge Street.

Construction workers who could reach downtown showed up to assess the damage. Steel girders had recently been erected for the new Masonic Temple at Shattuck and Bancroft Way. When the quake hit, the girders had slowly toppled, two of them falling through the roof of the neighboring University French Laundry at 2241 Shattuck and then striking the telephone company building at

ABOVE: *The earthquake opened up cracks in the Homestead Loan Association building at 2210 Shattuck Avenue.*

TOP LEFT: *The Barker Block building after the earthquake. It had been ready for occupancy when the quake struck. The damage was substantial. Owner J. L. Barker estimated the repairs at $5,000, which matched estimates of repairs to the Foy Block building across the street.*

BOTTOM LEFT: *The thriving Lorin district on Adeline Street in 1906, looking northeast toward the Berkeley hills. The district, popular among people who commuted to San Francisco, suffered some damage in the earthquake. The Key Route electric train in the foreground has a distinctive Brown Diamond roller pantograph, which connects the train to the electric lines. This invention ensured that electrical contact was maintained as the train went over bumps and grade changes. It was a vast improvement over the old "broomstick" trolley pole, which often needed to be reset.*

2239 Shattuck, just beyond the laundry. The two frightened switchboard operators on duty, Miss McGreer and Miss Young, remained at their stations, even though plaster was thrown from the bulging walls. Telephone service immediately went dead. An estimated 40 percent of the lines were down, and telephone poles all over town were toppled.

The Lorin district, south of downtown, also sustained heavy damage. The Loughhead and Armstrong Hardware building at 3226 Adeline Street was "way out of plumb" and the walls "cracked and shattered."[4]

Huge clouds of smoke from the San Francisco fires drifted eastward toward Berkeley. This photo was taken from the Southern Pacific freight yards, at Adeline and Oregon streets.

Chapter Four

THE UC CADETS SERVE IN SAN FRANCISCO

*A*lthough the UC cadets had been admired for many years, they faced increasing ridicule and disrespect from their fellow students at the turn of the century. Joining the military ranks had fallen out of political favor. The cadets hoped that a more friendly audience would show up for their annual inspections and maneuvers, starting at dawn on April 18.

As the proceedings got under way, the audience's attention was increasingly drawn to the sight of black smoke drifting toward them from San Francisco and the deep thuds of exploding dynamite. In San Francisco, desperate firemen were

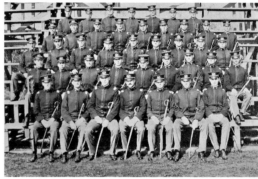

ABOVE: *The UC cadets as they appeared in the* 1908 *Blue and Gold yearbook.*

LEFT: *Cadet inspection day at UC Berkeley.*

Within an hour of the earthquake, fires in San Francisco began to rage out of control, despite the efforts of the city's fire department and the many volunteer hose carriers.

dynamiting buildings in the northern residential section and on Market Street in an attempt to stop the ever-growing fires from destroying even more structures. The constant booming distracted everyone from the cadets' drills. The ominous signs of catastrophe demanded an immediate response.

Rumors had already circulated around campus that the cadets would be asked to volunteer for service in San Francisco. When the San Francisco chief of police finally accepted Captain Nance's offer to send the cadets across the bay, word went out that all the cadets would be called into service. Even upperclassmen, who were not enrolled in the corps, showed up in their old uniforms. Told they would have to be self-sufficient once they left Berkeley, the cadets gathered

flasks, canteens, and blankets and flooded Berkeley grocers to buy canned meats, cheese, and crackers for personal emergency stashes. Nance lectured them that the duty ahead was serious and that anyone looking for a sightseeing trip should stay behind.

That afternoon, three battalions numbering six hundred in all boarded a ferry procured to rush them to the stricken city. The mood turned somber when they looked down at the black boxes of ammunition, which they might be forced to use in order to stop looters. "You are no more students but soldiers," Nance told his troops on the ferry ride across the bay. Despite these words, the young men could not have imagined what they were about to witness. Smoke soon blackened them as the ferry approached the dock in San Francisco.

Marching off the boat in formation, the cadets saw that entire sections of San Francisco lay in piles of smoking rubble. Lone walls stood at odd angles, sometimes crashing down spontaneously in clouds of dust. Horses still harnessed to wagons lay crushed under the rubble, as did the bodies of deceased residents. Frightened dogs ran through the streets, barking at a high pitch. The cadets were overpowered by the nearly unbearable intensity of the fires.

By early evening on April 18, the cadets, in dress uniform and armed with guns and live ammunition, were sent to patrol a large area of about eight by twenty-six blocks, bounded by Green and Waller streets on the north and south and Fillmore Street and Central Avenue on the east and west. As they approached Divisadero Street, they encountered frantic refugees fleeing the fires amid the succession of aftershocks, trying to escape the chaos, debris, dust, and death. No

ABOVE: *A UC cadet with his bayonet attached to his rifle.*

LEFT: *The scene that greeted the UC cadets arriving at the San Francisco Ferry Terminal. Ferries and ships struggled to accommodate refugees.*

On the morning of the earthquake, dead horses lay on San Francisco streets, hard and cold as stones.

A military unit, probably US Navy personnel from the cutter Bear, assembled for duty. The dog was one of hundreds wandering the city, lost in the aftermath of the catastrophe. The Fairmont Hotel is on the hill in the distance.

law enforcement units had been sent to this part of the city, and the cadets saw that many homes stood open and unprotected.

A guard post was set up on Golden Gate Avenue and used as a command center and jail. The cadets were assigned twelve-hour shifts. One of their duties was to help San Francisco firemen, many of whom worked steadily without rest or sleep. Some firemen were "half crazed from exhaustion and many of them [did] not seem to know what they [were] doing."[1] Blackened and sleepless, they were seen pulling burning shingles from roofs with their bare hands in a courageous attempt to stop the fire's advance.

The cadets tried to extinguish fires in shattered chimneys, which many agitated and frightened families persisted in using for warmth and cooking. The

Military men guard the 1000 block of Market Street as the fire rages.

The UC cadets arrived in San Francisco and marched in formation to their assigned sector.

It is likely that the military men in this photo are UC cadets, observing damage on Golden Gate Avenue near Hyde Street. Though this area was beyond the cadets' designated patrol area by nine blocks, many cadets were known to have traveled miles while off duty, often helping people or just walking to experience the enormity of the historic event they were a part of.

San Franciscans fled the furiously approaching fires and intense smoke and heat. Many headed toward the Ferry Building. Some of the men on the right walked in the direction of the smoke.

ABOVE: *A rare photo of San Francisco firemen rescuing an earthquake victim from the wreckage of the Brunswick Hotel at Sixth and Howard.*

TOP RIGHT: *San Franciscans stood by with their most precious belongings loaded, but hesitated to leave their homes until the approaching flames left them no choice. This view looks down Fell Street.*

The firemen of San Francisco desperately braved the fast-spreading flames and lack of water at the hydrants, often fighting fires with their bare hands and working until they dropped from exhaustion.

Two UC cadets on duty in San Francisco.

A cartoon of a UC cadet demanding that no gas or kerosene lights be used after the earthquake appeared in the 1908 Blue and Gold yearbook.

Not all the decisions cadets made were proper. One night, a lost poodle ran around terrified and barking. A cadet shot it for breaking the peace. A cartoon of the incident ran in the 1908 Blue and Gold yearbook. By then, the story had become legend.

William Keith's painting, A Memory of Berkeley, *survived the fires. Berkeley's best-known landscape painter had a studio on Pine Street in San Francisco. A friend broke down the door and was able to save only fourteen paintings before the fire approached. "I have too much to be thankful for to bemoan the loss of a few pictures and things," Keith was quoted in the* Oakland Enquirer *on May 8, 1906. "I am in perfect health and would rather paint than eat, so what is the loss of a few pictures."*

firefighters and their helpers often met with frustration when they discovered that hydrants lacked pressure or had run out of water, as the city's water mains were broken. Residents were asked to carry fire hoses and to help pump water from long-abandoned cisterns. Determined and creative firefighters and residents pumped sewer water and even threw wine and vinegar on the growing flames.

Those cadets not assigned specific duties were told to bivouac in an exposed empty lot. Lacking tents due to their hurried departure from Berkeley, they spread their blankets directly on the ground. The ashes and soot from the fires rained down on them, and they were often too agitated to rest. Many cadets complained of having insufficient food, but others shared what little they had with desperate residents who had lost their homes.

As underfed as they may have been, the cadets dutifully went on their assigned patrols. On Thursday, April 19, the day after the quake, Berkeley cadet Frank Simpson and a comrade responded to complaints that a dentist was charging homeless refugees the outrageous price of twenty-five cents for a cup of coffee. Upon investigating, Simpson found that the dentist was selling coffee

ABOVE: *A wealthy Pacific Heights resident used only the finest bricks for his new street kitchen.*

LEFT: *San Franciscans, prohibited from lighting indoor fires, had no trouble finding loose bricks to construct street kitchens. This one was in the residential area south of Market Street.*

made from government supplies. He confiscated the goods and demanded that, if the dentist sold any more provisions, he charge reasonable prices. When the dentist's neighbors heard of his profiteering, an angry crowd gathered and threatened to lynch him. Simpson shoved his way through the crowd and came to the dentist's rescue.[2]

On the evening of April 19, their second night of duty, the cadets were charged with helping local police and guards enforce the ordinance prohibiting the use of kerosene and gas lights. Kerosene lamps could easily be dropped or spilled by an aftershock, and gas lamps and lines could leak and explode—causing more fires and destroying more homes before the countless broken water mains could be repaired. The danger was so imminent that the city's policemen had been told to shoot any violators who did not immediately comply with their orders. Many cadets spent the night of April 19 marching up and down long staircases, banging on doors, and politely demanding that lights be extinguished. A number of residents gave the cadets meals, and grateful grocers handed them cigars.

One of the cadets' most difficult duties was preventing the sale of liquor, a measure that was viewed as essential for keeping order, but which resulted in

The Battle for
the Mark Hopkins Institute of Art

Railroad magnate Mark Hopkins built one of the most opulent mansions in San Francisco. Located at 975 California Street on Nob Hill, it had a commanding view of the city and bay. After Hopkins and his wife died, the building and its world-renowned art collection were endowed to the University of California, Berkeley, in 1893, which established an art institute in Hopkins's name.

The institute held shows in its exhibition hall and sponsored performances in its concert hall. Once a month, admission to the mansion was free to the public. Each year, thirty thousand people visited, and about two hundred students received their training from a faculty of nine.

Because of the high value of the art collection, fire protection for the mansion had been designed with the assistance of the city's fire department and head electrician. The university had received assurances that the safeguards were "absolutely complete."

After the April 18 earthquake, Nob Hill initally remained safe from the fires. But they soon began to close in and finally reached the institute, spreading along its eaves. The institute's employees, students sent from Berkeley, and sailors from the US Navy cutter *Bear* tried to find a safe place for the works of art. They took some to the basement of the nearby Flood mansion, which was made of masonry. More than a hundred paintings were cut from their frames and carried across the bay to the faculty room next to UC president Wheeler's office.

The fire destroyed not only the institute and its contents but irrevocably damaged the artworks in the Flood mansion basement. Of the statues, furniture, valuable books, and other items hurriedly piled on the Flood mansion lawn, only three statues survived the inferno.

The Mark Hopkins Institute, which crowned Nob Hill before it was destroyed by fire after the earthquake.

The gallery at the Mark Hopkins Institute.

The institute in ruins after the fire swept through the wooden building, destroying all but a few works of art.

The Flood mansion on California Street, near the Mark Hopkins Institute, after the fire. Statues rescued from the institute can be seen in this photo at the lower right corner of the lot.

A fire swarming into a narrow street in San Francisco.

Within hours after this photo was taken, the fires consumed all the structures in the foreground.

San Francisco's Ferry Plaza filled with refugees. Many horses were seized by the military for emergency duty, leaving residents to pull their own carriages. The crack in the cobblestone street was caused by the earthquake.

An April 20 photograph of refugees heading down Market Street toward the Ferry Building and a way out of San Francisco. Bricks littered the city.

Refugees took whatever they could carry as the Red Cross offered assistance.

Soldiers carrying dynamite into buildings. They destroyed the structures in an attempt to deny the fires fuel and create a firebreak.

ABOVE: *Two men pulling a trunk to the Ferry Building.*

RIGHT: *A 1906 postcard illustrated both the horror and the stoic humor of San Franciscans. Many residents had animals, and dogs, cats, and birds were common sights at refugee camps.*

UC cadet I. P. Aten, the corps' only casualty, was shot in the hip by troops while on duty.

the cadet corps' only casualty. According to one account, Corporal I. P. Aten was off duty when he passed a riot in a saloon on Fillmore Street. Compelled to see if his comrades needed assistance, he entered the saloon just as a volley was fired into the crowd without warning by regular troops also patrolling the area. Aten was wounded in the hip. He recovered only after a long convalescence at the Presidio's Letterman Hospital, but was left with a permanent limp.[3]

By Friday, April 20, layers of soot and dirt soiled the cadets' uniforms. Each hour, the fires were consuming an entire city block and leaving thousands more homeless, making for what the April 20 *Oakland Enquirer* called "an awful furnace of seething flame." To the people back in Berkeley and Oakland, San Francisco looked like an erupting volcano. "Light filled the sky for miles around. People in Sonoma and Santa Clara counties, fifty miles to the north and south, can remember a sky so luminous that you could read a newspaper at midnight."[4]

Tension was mounting as every car, horse, and wagon in the city was commandeered by city employees, the police, the US Army, and other officials to transport men, emergency supplies, casualties, and medical personnel. Dynamite and fuses were rushed to the areas where the fires raged. As the cadets attempted to regulate the traffic that clogged main streets, refugees streamed by, some pushing chairs filled with their possessions, the chair legs outfitted with roller-skates. Lacking horses, others used wheelbarrows. Children buckled under the weight of the bundles of bedding in their arms. One old woman carried a jar holding her goldfish.

Several observers noted that the incessant screeching sound of trunks being dragged along the pavement was the most recognizable sound of homeless residents fleeing their burning neighborhoods. The most astute among them pulled the trunks along the smooth rail tracks. San Franciscans were escaping not only the fires they feared would incinerate them and their possessions, but also the nightmarish sights of nearly unrecognizable charred bodies and crying babies sitting alone on the pavement. Some went to the train stations, others to the ferry docks, seeking a way to get to the East Bay. One reporter approached a San Francisco pioneer who pointed at the naked hills. "So it was when I came here," the old main said. "So bare. Only then it was green; now it is red."[5]

Off-duty cadets were so cold in their exposed lot that residents opened their cellars to them. They huddled together and tried to get some sleep. But they were too wound up and stayed awake, hurling jokes and witticisms through the darkness to distract themselves from their sore feet, scorched nasal passages, and exhaustion. When some cadets were supposed to be resting, they were found to have walked miles to deliver telegrams for refugees and to offer help to women and children.

As the sun rose on Saturday, April 21, the fires were under control and the cadets began to relax a little. One found an open dry goods store where some of the men bought a change of clothes. Many purchased pencils and paper so they could write friends and family in Berkeley. They thought they would be on duty for at least a week and wanted to share their experiences.

By noon the whole camp received orders from General Frederick Funston of the Presidio to return to Berkeley. When the earthquake hit, General Funston had been downtown at his home at Washington and Jones streets and unable to reach the troops in the Presidio by telegraph, so he sent messengers summoning them to the areas of the city that needed immediate assistance. He also

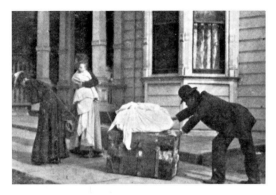

Fleeing San Francisco with possessions hastily packed into trunks was made much more difficult by the city's hills and the pervasive smoke.

Refugees, many driving horse-drawn carriages, converged on the Ferry Building and waited for their chance to escape the city.

Stunned San Francisco residents huddling in Lafayette Square.

called for men and supplies from every nearby base—Angel Island, Mare Island, Monterey, and elsewhere—who began arriving as fast as they could. When General Funston felt the numbers of his forces were adequate, he requested the UC cadets' departure because of their lack of supplies and a concern that they might be needed in Berkeley. The cadets were marched down Golden Gate Avenue to Market Street and back to the ferry.

As the cadets passed a cluster of improvised shacks operating as humble sidewalk cafés, one elbowed the man to his left and motioned with a slight tilt

Near Left: *General Frederick Funston issued commands to his troops by messengers.*

Far Left: *Market Street in ruins, photographed from the top of the Ferry Building. This is the scene witnessed by the cadets as they made their way to the ferry that would take them back to Berkeley on April 21.*

of his head. Most of the shacks had slogans chalked on their sides. This particular one read, "Eat, Drink, and Be Merry, for Tomorrow We May Have To Go To Oakland." Another seemed a more appropriate farewell: "CRASHED, BUT NOT CRUSHED. DOWN, BUT NOT OUT!" By evening, the cadets were back home in Berkeley, resting their swollen feet and still coughing from the smoke they had inhaled over the previous few days.

Many San Francisco residents were so impressed with the cadets' behavior and grateful for their help that they petitioned for their return. Two hundred San Franciscans wrote a joint letter, dated May 4, 1906, to UC president Benjamin Ide Wheeler. They spoke of the invaluable protection provided by the cadets and of their firm belief that through the cadets' "innumerable acts of

A Cadet Writes His Sister

UC Berkeley cadet Charles Noyes Forbes wrote his younger sister, Carrie Hyde Forbes, after he and other cadets returned to Berkeley, having spent the days after the earthquake helping San Francisco residents. He addresses her by her childhood nickname, Kye. A sophomore in 1906, Charles lived in a boardinghouse at 2456 Derby Street.

UC cadet Charles Noyes Forbes, who served in San Francisco in the aftermath of the earthquake.

Apr. 22, 1906

Dear Kye:

At 5:15 Wed morning we had a tremendous earthquake shock & several smaller ones which knocked down every chimney and a great many brick buildings here, but this was insignificant to what I saw in San Francisco. Thursday morning I went to Frisco in my cadet uniform which passed me anywhere. Went all over and saw the big sky scrapes cracked & all tumbled too [sic] pieces by the earthquake, but its affects [sic] were almost obliterated by the fierce fire that followed. The greater part of the city is gone. We went along the fire line & helped the police & soldiers drive on the frenzied crowd bust up liquor places Etc. For the last 3 days I've been doing guard duty. We are on an equal footing with the regular soldiers and marines. The police have no authority whatsoever as the city is under martial law. Our duty was to break up all saloons where liquor was sold in most cases making the proprietor smash his own bottles on the curb stone, to prevent looting & not to allow the people to have fires & lights in the houses. There are lots of provisions coming into the city so there will be no famine. We came back yesterday foot sore but feeling fine & will do police duty in Berkeley, tame after Frisco. Hundreds of people are coming over here & all the houses are full. Uncle George has 3 Russians & a lunatic. The University buildings are untouched not even a chimney down, not a crack in the Amphitheatre [sic], but not a building stands at Stanford. All exercises are suspended until the exes, but it seems unjust to have them a[t] such a time at all.

Forgot to say that one of our fellows was shot in the hip. It looks serious for him. Well I'll [sic] guess I'll have to stop now & write again later. So sending love I remain

Yours Aff,

Charles

Courtesy of the Paul and Sandra Little History Collection.

kindness and never failing courage the loss of life was greatly lessened."[6]

Before serving in San Francisco, the cadets had felt disparaged by much of the student body. Upon their return, they were surprised that the bashing they once took had been "left with the other ashes in San Francisco," replaced by a newfound respect from their peers.[7]

At least two cadets, however, were disciplined by their superiors. Just over a week after the earthquake, cadet Captain Chee Soo Lowe was demoted to the rank of private by Captain Nance and university president Wheeler. No reason for the action was offered in local newspapers, and no records remain of the incident. He had been the only Asian officer in the corps. Cadet Frank Simpson, who had saved the profiteering dentist from an angry mob, was also in trouble. He had expected to receive a commendation, but was shocked when commanding officers, upon investigating his actions, determined that he had gone beyond his appointed patrol territory. Simpson was in danger of losing his rank.

Despite the high praise the cadet corps received, they bore the brunt of some malicious and serious accusations against them. Reports spread in San Francisco that the cadets had been called back to Berkeley because they were shooting too many people without uttering the customary "halt!" When Colonel Force, one of the cadets' commanders, heard about this, he was furious. He explained to reporters that no complaints had ever been leveled against his men. He further noted that the cadets were volunteers who had left Berkeley on almost no notice. They had not had enough time to bring an adequate supply of tents, blankets, and food rations and were exposed to the elements for three days while serving twelve-hour shifts. Vigorously defending the cadets from charges that they had fired unnecessarily on San Francisco residents, Force mentioned that only one person had been killed. The Japanese man, whom the colonel referred to by using the pejorative slang of the era, had refused to extinguish a light. The cadets had been following strict orders to demand immediate compliance that no fires of any kind be lit.

In his fury to defend the cadets, the colonel noted that the city had been filled with regulars—soldiers from the army and other services—as well as militiamen, or guardsmen, from other parts of the state, who intimidated the cadets. "They were afraid of the regulars," the colonel said, "who in many cases

Caricature of Colonel Force of the UC cadets, from the 1908 Blue and Gold *yearbook.*

RIGHT: *Pen and ink cartoon of Captain Nance, who arranged for the cadets to volunteer in San Francisco, from the 1908 Blue and Gold UC Berkeley yearbook. He was one of the commanders of the corps while they were on duty in the city.*

A lone cadet on the UC campus.

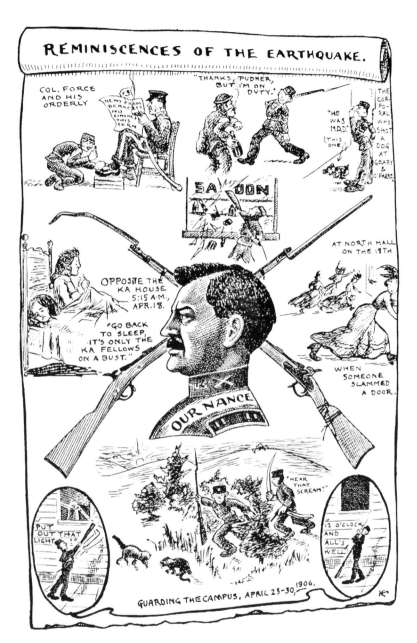

were howling drunk. So drunk were they that when a detail of four men were out getting food for the people they fired on them and shot a private named Alten [Aten] in the thigh." The colonel asserted that the cadet Aten had been wounded by drunken regular troops who had fired on the cadets without warning, not, as the *1908 Blue and Gold* yearbook described, by walking into a saloon fracas. Colonel Force told how his men had to lock a number of drunken regulars up in the guardhouse to "keep them out of trouble."

Force accused the police of starting the rumors. There was much tension between law enforcement agencies—cadets, regulars, militiamen, and police. On April 20, San Francisco policeman Joseph Myers was bayoneted and killed by a national guardsman over a dispute about authority. Not long afterward, a riot nearly broke out when a militiaman aimed his rifle at a policeman. Six nearby policemen pounced on the man and disarmed, subdued, and then released him—but without his rifle. The regular army troops called the militiamen "a pack of kids."

A prominent San Francisco policeman said of the cadets, "These young fellows are causing no end of trouble. They hold up police and cover them with their rifles before saying a word. Our men don't know what moment they will be shot. Something should be done. We have no trouble with the men of the regular army, for they know their business."[8]

The public airing of grievances diminished within several days after the cadets returned to Berkeley. Authorities and residents on both sides of the bay faced other problems that would consume their attention and resources.

People gathered in the East Bay hills and flatlands to view the fires consuming San Francisco and watch the arrival of ferryboats overflowing with refugees.

Chapter Five

REFUGEES DELIVERED
TO THE OPEN ARMS OF BERKELEY

While the UC cadets were policing San Francisco and aiding the city's residents, Berkeleyans were watching the fires from across the bay. Donald McLaughlin (for whom UC Berkeley's McLaughlin Hall is named), then a child, stood outside his home at 1629 Euclid Avenue for three nights, beginning on April 18, and watched the waves of fires wash over the city. "It was a worrisome three days," he recalled, "while we watched San Francisco burn, especially at night as the flames advanced from the central region behind Goat Island [now called Yerba Buena Island] to wider and wider fringes that by the end of the third day made us think there was nothing left of the city."[1]

While McLaughlin was staring out across the bay, refugees were fleeing the city, many of them headed for Berkeley and other East Bay towns. Among them was Mrs. Maria Lenskin, a widow, who resided with her young daughter, Vera, and two dogs, at 1770 Taylor Street. Maria was friends with famous painters, newspapermen, and what one writer called "extreme liberals" of the day. At 5:14 a.m. on April 18, Maria, still dressed in the clothes she had worn to the opera the evening before, was sitting in her living room with friends. By the first night after the quake, she and Vera were sleeping on blankets in a vacant lot at Taylor and Union streets, having loaded all they could carry into Vera's doll carriage. One rescued item was the urn holding her deceased husband's ashes. Her dogs, a Russian wolfhound and a mutt, stood guard.[2]

As the fires spread and smoke blackened the sky, Maria and her entourage sought refuge at Harbor View Park, an amusement park at the foot of Baker and Jefferson streets. Early arrivals set up house in tents provided by the army. Less

Children waited along with their parents at ferries, camps, and food lines. In the chaos of the fires and the crush of the crowds, many children were separated from their families.

As neighborhoods burned, San Franciscans rushed to the ferries leaving the city. Crews frantically loaded as many people as the boats could accommodate.

Refugees arriving in Oakland by ferry had to hire rigs, often at extortionate prices, to take them to the homes of friends or relatives.

Woman waiting with her belongings at the Ferry Building. Despite the scenes of panic throughout the city, many San Franciscans displayed great calm and fortitude. One observer who noted this was Jack London, sent to the city to report on the earthquake's aftermath by Collier's magazine. London's account, entitled "The Story of an Eyewitness," appeared in the May 5, 1906 edition.

Desperate to reach other destinations, refugees in Oakland climbed on top of trains when the cars were full. The railroads offered free transportation.

Refugees scrambled to the Ferry Building and then to safety in the East Bay.

Downtown Oakland swelled with refugees who arrived by train and ferry. Many traveled by streetcar to Berkeley.

fortunate refugees made their own with blankets and broom handles, surrounding their makeshift shelters with trunks, chairs, birdcages, and the other meager possessions they had managed to save. As sparks fell down on the camp, rumors spread that a nearby gas tank would explode. Maria gathered her daughter, dogs, and belongings and fled. They wound up at the harbor, where she was given permission to board a government ship along with hundreds of other San Franciscans bound for the East Bay and safety.

Trains teeming with traumatized men, women, and children, weighted down by their possessions, hurriedly left San Francisco from the Southern Pacific terminal at Third and Townsend streets. The trains barreled south to San Jose, then headed north to Oakland. Numerous refugees continued on to the Berkeley Station at Shattuck Avenue and Center Street.

The Southern Pacific Railroad also loaded railcars onto special ferries designed with tracks on their decks. Both the railcar ferries and the passenger ferries departed the city for the Souther Pacific Oakland terminal at the bottom of Seventh Street, where many refugees boarded trains for Berkeley. The Key Route trains had stopped running when the power was shut off, just minutes after the quake, but the Key Route ferries took passengers to the mole south of Berkeley. From there, refugees had to walk almost four miles to the functioning trains at Sixteenth Street in Oakland.

San Franciscans who took ferries described how thousands of panicky people, many with tear-stained faces, pushed each other aside to get on the boats. "Fighting my way to the gate like the others," one passenger later recalled, "the thought came into my mind of what rats in a trap we were. Had I not been a strong man I should certainly have been killed."

Many refugees arriving in Berkeley still wore their sleeping attire, having never returned to their burning or crumbling homes. Deprived of sleep and food, they were sapped of energy. As they stumbled from the trains, many looked for a patch of grass, collapsed, and fell asleep. Others spoke in a solemn hush about the unbearable heat of the fire. One man told of witnessing a building that had not yet been touched by the advancing conflagration burst into flames, as if by spontaneous combustion.

They could not believe what had just happened to them. The night before, they had been living their normal lives. Now they stood with nothing, in Berkeley, which seemed a continent away from their homes across the bay.

Despite their exhaustion, they wanted to tell their stories. "The house was shaken as a terrier shakes a rat," one San Franciscan related. Many said that the shaking ended with a vicious snap. Others remembered the startling silence that came after the deafening roar of crashing buildings stopped. Ng Poon Chew, editor of a San Francisco daily Chinese language newspaper, described the horrors of the fire: "The atmosphere in San Francisco is most terrible. The gases, the smoke, the cinders, the copper sun, the haze, made it a hideous dream."[3]

One young man, recognizing his neighbor, put his arm around the other's shoulder to comfort him and said, "Hello, Billy. What have you got left?" "My health," the other responded. A reporter asked a woman how she fared. "Oh,

Once refugees set foot in Oakland, they needed to figure out where to go next. Some just walked around in a daze.

This woman was probably dressed in men's clothing because she had lost everything and had nothing to wear. During the relief effort, women were often given men's clothing, which was in more plentiful supply.

Passengers going up the gangplanks were still in the clothes they wore when the earthquake struck, whether their finest attire or their pajamas and nightgowns.

Water wagons sprinkling the dirt of Shattuck Avenue around 60th Street to keep the dust down.

losers!" the woman responded. "Like the rest—there ain't any winners in this game."[4]

Charles Huggins, a Berkeley engineer, described the masses of afflicted San Franciscans: "The refugees didn't seem in their right minds—they seemed stunned, particularly in what they saved. One carried nothing else that I could see but a length of stovepipe. Practically everybody seemed to be carrying a bird. They felt the shock and took only, I suppose, what first came to their minds."[5]

Looking back seventy-five years later, Herbert Kling, seven years old at the time, remembered his grandfather arriving in Berkeley from San Francisco. "He brought the most ridiculous things. They used to have these tree frogs in glass cylinders that they used to predict the weather. Grandfather also had a hat that he wore to funerals and such and he just had to have that. So he came over with a tree frog and a top hat."[6]

Some survivors were so rattled they could not remember the names of the streets where they had lived for years or the city they wanted to go to after leaving San Francisco. A reporter was struck by one woman who kept repeating "No one was killed, but what am I to do?" over and over again. Another wrote, "The pity is for those who suffer in stolid silence. Poor, dazed and stricken people who only stand and suffer. No messages for them. Only the kind word of the relief worker. Let us be generous with these words."[7]

Distributing water from a water wagon at a San Francisco refugee camp.

President Theodore Roosevelt sent a telegram to California governor George Pardee within hours of the earthquake. The telegram's contents sounded more like words of reassurance sent to a stunned friend than an executive message: "It was difficult to credit the news of the calamity that had fallen on San Francisco. I feel the greatest concern for you and the people, not only of San Francisco, but of California in the terrible disaster. You will let me know if there is anything that the government can do."[8]

President Theodore Roosevelt.

PREPARING FOR DOOM

Following the 1906 earthquake, a religious sect in Berkeley was convinced that the end of the world had come. According to the reminiscences of Janette Howard Wallace, daughter of UC Berkeley architect John Galen Howard, the group, dressed in white robes, remained in the hills for several days and sang hymns.

When nothing happened, they "very sheepishly had to come back down again when everything had quieted down." According to Wallace, "they were sure the end of the world had come and they were the only ones who would be taken off to heaven."

This was not the first time people in the East Bay interpreted an earthquake as a religious event. On April 14, 1890, the world was supposed to end in a large earthquake. More than two hundred people, mostly Swedes and Norwegians, retreated to a canyon just east of the Berkeley hills and set up tents in anticipation of the cataclysm. They prayed, sang, and experienced visions, convinced that they would be saved as San Francisco and Oakland perished. April 14 came and went and they felt nothing, yet tried to persuade themselves that San Francisco and Oakland had been destroyed while they had been spared. The group mounted the ridge, expecting to see the Pacific Ocean lapping at the hills. The world was unchanged, and everyone went home, convinced that their prayers had made the difference.

CLEANING UP SAN FRANCISCO

Both skilled and day laborers were needed to clear rubble from San Francisco streets, repair rail tracks, and restore utilities, as well as demolish severely damaged buildings. Tens of thousands, including men from the East Bay, were hired within days of the earthquake. They wanted a firsthand look at the disaster as well as a chance to earn some money.

Paul Spenger, of the Spenger's Restaurant family, had spent three days in San Francisco lugging fire hoses at the direction of the military. He returned to the city when he learned about some construction work. Paid $3.50 per day, he labored to clear the debris from collapsed brick buildings. He was ordered to climb up three and a half stories in the Merchants Exchange Building at 465 California Street and knock down a fifteen-foot section of wall dangling over a bank vault in the same building. Other workers, fearing the wall's imminent collapse, refused to attempt it.

There were no stairs or ladders to reach this section, but this did not deter Spenger. "I climbed the pipe," he said, "and when I got to the hole in the wall the pipe fell. And I hollered, 'Look out below.' Everybody got out of the road, and I cleared all the bricks away and I pulled the thing down. Then, to get down, I fell down about a story and a half to the next building, went through a skylight, and landed in the next floor."

By the end of the year, the Merchants Exchange was rebuilt.

Thousands of men were hired to clear debris from San Francisco streets.

From the recent massive fires in Chicago and Baltimore, San Franciscans knew not to open their safes right after the fires, as the fresh air rushing into the hot interior would cause the contents to burst into flames. Experts transported the safes to safety or monitored them until they were cool enough to open.

The Merchants Exchange Building at 465 California Street, the tallest building on the right side of the street. It is still at this site.

The area near the Berkeley Station, where refugees arrived by Southern Pacific and Key Route trains. The Southern Pacific depot, at lower right, was at Shattuck Avenue and Center Street. The three-story wooden Odd Fellows Hall, across the street, at Shattuck Avenue and Addison Street, was the site of an emergency hospital. To its left, on the northeast corner of Shattuck and Addison, was the Mason-McDuffie building, where the Berkeley Relief Committee was formed on April 18, 1906.

Chapter Six

THE RELIEF EFFORT

*B*erkeley responded with remarkable speed to help the San Franciscans streaming into town. F. W. Foss, president of the Berkeley Chamber of Commerce, called for a town meeting to decide what could be done to assist the victims. The meeting, held the morning of April 18 at the chamber offices in the First National Bank at Shattuck Avenue and Center Street, was packed with concerned Berkeleyans. The attendees quickly set up a citizen Relief Committee, to be housed at the Mason-McDuffie Real Estate office at Shattuck and Center, near the downtown train station. This convenient location would allow relief workers to meet the refugees as they stepped off the trains and to provide them with shelter, food, and clothing, along with any medical attention they might need. The Reverend E. L. Parsons, rector at St. Mark's Church, was made chairman of the Relief Committee.

The Reverend E. L. Parsons of St. Mark's Church was appointed chairman of Berkeley's Relief Committee.

Many subcommittees, called departments, were formed to handle health, housing, and other tasks. Berkeley residents from all walks of life—church leaders, university professors, veterans, and leaders from the business community, as well as city officials—came forward to head the departments. Duncan McDuffie, of Mason-McDuffie Real Estate, took charge of the Office Department, which organized a clearing center responsible for receiving the refugees and transporting them to their designated housing. He was also responsible for disseminating information, such as posting notices about the need for housing in Oakland newspapers. Frank Wilson, chairman of the Finance Department, began accepting contributions in cash and provisions. He proceeded to collect approximately $3,000 in the hours just after the earthquake.

An Amusement Park Becomes a Refugee Camp

Shortly after it opened in May of 1903, Idora Park became a popular weekend attraction for Berkeleyans and other East Bay residents. The park's amusements—including a large theater, a skating rink, a merry-go-round, a roller coaster, picnic grounds, gardens, and a zoo—occupied about three and a half square blocks between Fifty-sixth and Fifty-eighth streets, and Shattuck and Telegraph avenues. The park was built by real estate magnate Borax Smith, owner of the San Francisco, Oakland & San Jose Railway (commonly known as the Key Route), in order to create demand for his electric trains on weekends.

When the earthquake hit on April 18, the company offered to house San Francisco refugees at the park. Early that afternoon, tents were set up in the open spaces, and cots and bedding were brought to the theater and other buildings. By evening, hundreds of hot meals were prepared, and soup, bread and butter, and coffee were distributed to help comfort the refugees. Berk York, the park's manager, never turned anyone away if space was available.

On April 18 the park put up 245 refugees in the theater. An aftershock later that night caused them to panic and run out of the building. It was some time before they could bring themselves to go back inside. At one point, the federal government estimated that 2,500 refugees were being sheltered in the park. A few weeks after the quake, the remaining refugees were transferred to the centralized camps run by the Oakland Relief Committee.

Idora Park looking toward the hills. The main entrance was by the streetcar stop on Telegraph Avenue, in the center right.

When the park reopened, it had a new feature, the Idora Park Opera Company, whose performers included members of San Francisco's famed Tivoli Theater. Many members of the orchestra were from the UC Berkeley Symphony Orchestra. The company debuted on May 17 with Gilbert and Sullivan's *The Mikado*.

ABOVE: *A tent erected for earthquake refugees who fled to Idora Park.*

TOP RIGHT: *The theater at Idora Park. Cots were set up in the building to provide emergency shelter. Fatty Arbuckle performed in the theater. Lon Cheney was an electrician there. Charlie Chaplin was rumored to have visited and worked in the park.*

BOTTOM RIGHT: *In June, after Idora Park reopened, visitors flocked to the Fabiola Fête, a special event.*

LEFT: *Acting Berkeley mayor Francis Ferrier.*
RIGHT: *UC history professor Bernard Moses.*

UC Berkeley president Benjamin Ide Wheeler.

The purpose of the Oriental Department was to care for segregated groups of Chinese and Japanese refugees. This was an era when anti-Asian sentiments ran high, fueled by fear that white citizens would lose their jobs or that Asians would spread contagious diseases. There was even an Anti-Asian League whose presence in Berkeley was condoned. As word arrived that the San Francisco jails had been emptied of prisoners (as it turned out, they were being transferred as the fires devoured the city), a Protection Department was formed to deal with what was described as a "tendency toward lawlessness that follows such great confusion, excitement and disease." Acting Mayor Francis Ferrier, in one of the few other official acts the Berkeley government took, appointed a "committee of safety" to do whatever necessary to maintain order, enforce sanitary regulations (posted in English, German, Spanish, Italian, and other languages), and generally guard the public welfare.

The heads of the departments formed an executive committee that met twice daily in the first few days after the earthquake. To oversee the citywide effort, the Relief Committee took on the job of supervising the work of local organizations such as churches and fraternal groups. The Relief Committee, in turn, coordinated its tasks with the city and the university through a Town and University Committee (formed by appointment of the mayor). All important questions involving the relief efforts were referred to this committee. Its members included UC Berkeley president Benjamin Ide Wheeler, Reverend Parsons, Frank Wilson, and UC history professor Bernard Moses. Little time had been wasted in creating a well-organized relief machinery that did not hesitate to make its own laws and enforce them. Within a week of the quake, Wheeler described, almost jocularly, the situation in Berkeley to President Theodore Roosevelt as "practically a government by vigilance committee."[1]

Before the initial Relief Committee meeting on April 18 adjourned, thirty-one households offered to shelter refugees, whether in a spare room or on a shared couch. Guy Chick, a former Berkeley building inspector, volunteered a ten-room house. By 2 a.m. on the morning of April 19, more than three hundred homes were prepared for the displaced San Francisco residents, along with damaged Stiles Hall and the Native Sons' Hall at 2108 Shattuck Avenue. With accommodations found for eight hundred refugees, the Housing Department

Berkeley Daily Gazette, *April 27, 1906.*

BOARD WANTED

San Francisco People are beginning to apply to us for Board. This must be at very reasonable rates to meet existing conditions.

NOW IS THE TIME
TO ATTRACT DESIRABLE
RESIDENTS TO BERKELEY

All Boarding Houses or Private Families please list accommodations with us **at once.** We undertake this work without expense to you.

Berkeley Releif Committee

210 Center Street   Corner Shattuck Avenue

was just reaching its stride. Local real estate firms provided men and rigs to transport refugees to their assigned housing.

Hundreds of frightened San Francisco refugees spent the first night after the earthquake in the Berkeley hills, suffering through the chilly night without enough provisions rather than take shelter in Berkeley buildings that might be damaged by aftershocks. Eleven women reportedly gave birth in the hills that night, with no medical assistance. Nine of them were said to have died. As the sun rose on April 19 over the hills and illuminated the clouds of smoke that had

Berkeley Daily Gazette, *n.d.*

A refugee begins her day by tending to her animals.

blown east across the bay, the hungry, sleepless refugees staggered down in search of assistance.

Starting late that morning, a torrent of refugees flooded the town, most of them arriving by train from Oakland. This pace continued all day, making the night of April 19 particularly hectic for relief workers trying to place and feed an estimated seven thousand refugees. Vacant rooms became impossible to find. The need was so great that almost every Berkeley household provided accommodations to friends or strangers from San Francisco. UC professors took in homeless San Franciscans, and even fraternity and sorority members gave up their lodging for use by the refugees. Everyone was instructed to keep the refugees inside rather than let them loiter in front of houses and other buildings. Maria Lenskin and her daughter, who had traveled to the East Bay on a government ship, were among the more fortunate refugees. Their ship, like most all the other vessels leaving San Francisco for the East Bay, arrived at Oakland's waterfront. There, Red Cross volunteers met the refugees as they disembarked and interviewed them about their needs. Mrs. Lenskin told the workers that she had a brother, Anthony Verdi, who lived at 1145 Oxford Street in Berkeley. They suggested that she go there, but before transportation could be arranged all the way to her brother's home, Lenskin and her daughter slept on cots at Berkeley's Trinity Methodist Episcopal Church at Allston Way and Fulton Street. She still had the possessions she took from San Francisco, including the urn with her husband's ashes. Lenskin finally made it to her brother's house, where a tent was set up to shelter her and her daughter. She eventually bought a house at 1347 La Loma Avenue, becoming one of many San Franciscans to settle permanently in Berkeley.[2]

Relief workers realized that they needed to help friends and family contact the refugees. On Friday, April 20, as the number of refugees in Berkeley reached ten to twelve thousand, a register was set up at relief headquarters. Refugees signed in and noted where they would be housed. If they had not yet been given housing, they still posted their names, and perhaps a message, so loved ones would know that they had survived and were in Berkeley. The register led to many reunions.

One of the trains that arrived on Thursday, April 19, just after noon, was

ANOTHER VICTIM OF THE QUAKE

Chinese Child of Four Years Dies as a Result of Sickness Caused by Fright by Temblor.

Lau Big York, a Chinese child of four years, died at 2033 Blake street yesterday as a result of sickness brought on by fright. The child was living with his parents in Chinatown, in San Francisco, at the time of the earthquake, and was brought by them to this city when so many Chinese refugees fled to Berkeley. The child has been ill ever since and passed away early yesterday evening.

Berkeley Daily Gazette, May 29, 1906.

packed with refugees of Chinese and Japanese descent, the two predominant Asian populations in Berkeley. Filing off the train, they congregated on Addison Street, filling an entire block near Shattuck Avenue. This group and many other Chinese and Japanese refugees were soon confined to the Dwight Way district, which already had a significant Asian population. Many found housing with friends or relatives around town, but those who didn't would have to be provided with housing fast. To that end, attention focused on a known gambling house, Ge Thang's, at the corner of Shattuck Avenue and Blake Street. A year earlier, Berkeley police marshal August Vollmer had raided the place for its gambling and opium operation above the first-floor grocery store. Now, during a city emergency, Ge Thang's was quickly set up as a nursery for about forty children up to the age of six.

Nearly all of the Asian refugees were from San Francisco's dense Chinatown, which had burnt to the ground with little warning. Following the earthquake, Asian refugees fanned out over the East Bay and beyond. By April 22, more than twenty thousand Chinese refugees were packed into Oakland's Chinatown, around Eighth and Ninth streets, near Lake Merritt. Three thousand reached

San Francisco's Chinatown before the earthquake.

Sacramento, one thousand Fresno, and another thousand Stockton.

Estimates of the Chinese refugees in Berkeley constantly varied. Between April 22 and 26, five hundred to a thousand Chinese refugees were living in the Alcatraz Avenueanywhere from ten to thirty-five segregated camps. Another five to eight hundred were staying in private houses. In the week after the earthquake, three UC professors attempted to address the needs of these

Chinatown in ruins after the earthquake.

refugees. A Chinese Office and a Chinese Employment Bureau were set up with the help of twenty-four Chinese students.[3]

On April 30, a segregated outdoor camp with twenty tents and potential accommodations for up to four hundred Chinese refugees was hurriedly established at University Avenue and Sacramento Street. A committee was formed with Thomas Hing as chairman. C. Y. Cheng was named secretary of the camp. The committee's members and the camp's staff of five met daily at 7 p.m. at the Chinese Students' Club at 2316 Fulton Street. The camp also held the main food supply for the Chinese refugees in Berkeley. Rice was initially brought from San Francisco by the ship *Mongolia.* The Relief Committee then took over providing food until the end of the month, when the Chinese consulate began sending rice. The University and Sacramento camp was not well liked by the Chinese refugees, and by May 3 only thirty people were utilizing the facility, and thirty sacks of rice remained in the club's basement.[4]

A local organization, the Chinese Empire Relief Association, specialized in the concerns of the Chinese refugees. A UC Berkeley sophomore, O. S. Lee, a Chinese American, acted as the association's interpreter. "What we are lacking

A father and his children in Chinatown before the earthquake, photographed by Arnold Genthe.

A segregated East Bay refugee camp for Chinese and Chinese American refugees from San Francisco.

most is rice," he said. "If we have plenty of that, we can do without much of anything else, but so far we have been unable to get it, most of our stores of it having been burned in San Francisco." Lee went on to explain how the community had sent telegrams back east, but knew that help would be awhile in coming. American relief workers had promised assistance as soon as possible, but Lee politely accepted the reality of the white Americans' view of the Chinese as outsiders. "Of course we know that they have their hands full, you might say, with their own people," he said. "We see, however, that in times like this there is no race prejudice, and we want to tell you that we are very, very thankful for the kindly spirit that is shown by all towards us. We wish you would say that particularly for us."[5]

Although the Chinese were in segregated camps, the accommodations, meals, and clothing given to them were the same as provided to refugees in other local camps. In May, after the US Army took over relief operations, the

The main refugee camp at UC Berkeley's California Field, now the site of the Hearst Gymnasium.

same government officials inspected and approved all camps and, by all accounts, never received any formal complaints from Asian refugees about maltreatment. Even representatives of the Chinese government accepted the segregation of Asians without question. Reports later issued by the US government stated that the refugees in the Asian camps were better at surviving on minimal provisions than the other refugees in the Berkeley, Oakland, and Alameda camps. Being self-sufficient, the Asian refugees did not like the idea of charity and were among the first to procure new jobs or take advantage of opportunities to improve their situation.

Liang Cheng, China's minister in Washington, D.C., said, "We are grateful for the attention our people are receiving."[6] In May, a couple of weeks after making this statement, he visited Oakland on behalf of the emperor to observe how the Chinese were being cared for and to take measures ensuring that they found permanent housing.

Approximately a thousand Japanese refugees were counted in Berkeley on April 29. Half of them were housed in private homes, and two hundred were being helped at The Friends Church, at Haste near Shattuck. The Japanese initially organized their own relief efforts, but during the first week in May the

chairman of the Japanese Relief Association declared that fifty Japanese were in distress and sought outside help. His plea was answered by Berkeley's relief organization.

While the citizen Relief Committee and its various departments were hard at work downtown the day of the earthquake, UC Berkeley quickly began to organize its relief efforts. Stiles Hall was made headquarters for the university's relief workers. Assembled there, instructors and students came up with a systematic plan to receive San Francisco refugees who needed housing and other assistance. Although they oversaw their own operations, they worked closely with the Relief Committee and city officials from April 18 forward.

Accommodations, referred to as sanitary camps, were set up on campus by people with expertise in modern medical and sanitation practices. Tents for families were erected on California Field (now Hearst Gym). The baseball field (now occupied by the Life Sciences Building) became the site of hundreds of tents for male refugees. A deep layer of straw was first laid down to help pad the ground. Not only were unmarried men kept segregated, but they were under armed guard after dark. In case of rain, the men were allowed in Harmon Gym. Single

The old UC Berkeley baseball field before the earthquake, where local boys and men would devise ways to watch the ballgames, in spite of the high fence. North Hall is visible above the baseball field. The field, located where the Life Sciences Building now stands, housed male refugees in tents after the earthquake.

Harmon Gymnasium, UC Berkeley, where bathing and laundry facilities were utilized by the refugees.

Hearst Hall, UC Berkeley, Channing Way and College Avenue, where single women refugees were housed and fed.

The north end of the main floor of UC Berkeley's Hearst Hall, circa 1901.

women were housed and fed at Hearst Hall at Channing Way and College Avenue. A medical and obstetrical hospital was established there as well. The bathing facilities at the men's and women's gymnasiums were turned over for use by the refugees, and laundry facilities were established in Harmon Gym.

Kitchens, both indoor and outdoor, sprung up on campus to feed those in need. A large one was located south of the baseball field under the oaks, not far from sculptor Douglas Tilden's statue of football players. Elsewhere on campus, twenty cooking ranges were set up under a stand of oaks. Volunteers, mostly

ABOVE: *The campus's peaceful setting soothed refugees' nerves.*

LEFT: *An outdoor kitchen and dining area at UC Berkeley. Nearby stood the well-known statue of football players by Douglas Tilden, who attended the School for the Deaf and Blind in Berkeley.*

female students, served the hot food in a huge tent filled with tables. Herbert Kling later recalled how his parents, who owned a grocery and delicatessen at Shattuck Avenue and Dwight Way, served lines of refugees "bean sandwiches prepared from pots assembled near Strawberry Creek on the UC Berkeley campus."[7]

Utility companies provided electricity and gas to the camps on the UC campus, as well as other East Bay camps, free of charge, and the Contra Costa Water Company installed water lines for cooking, drinking, and bathing, and separate lines for sewage. The Sunset Telephone and Telegraph Company laid telephone lines to all locations where relief work was carried out, making sure that the best phones available were in the field.

The parklike atmosphere of the campus was soothing to the shaken refugees who arrived after visiting the Relief Committee headquarters. "Berkeley is looked upon as a haven of peace and rest from the terrible scenes and disasters in the doomed city," the April 20 *Oakland Tribune* reported. Some people, however, especially male refugees, did not feel comfortable living under the regimented

ABOVE: *The ranchlands of north Berkeley, which later became the neighborhood of Northbrae.*

ABOVE LEFT: *Refugees who preferred to avoid the sanitary camps and their regulations made their way north, settling beyond city limits in what became known as Tin Can Town.*

conditions of the sanitary camps. Those wanting less supervision went beyond the northern city limits at Eunice Street to the farms and ranchlands that a few years later would become the Northbrae, Cragmont, and Thousand Oaks neighborhoods. Unofficial, unregulated camps grew up in the open fields, filled with small shelters made of sheet metal and tarps. These camps remained until late fall, and during this period, the area was known as Tin Can Town.[8]

Many organizations, churches, charitable groups, commercial establishments, and individuals initiated their own relief efforts under the supervision of the Relief Committee. Trinity Methodist Episcopal Church, on Allston Way at Fulton Street, took in more than a hundred refugees. The Elks Lodge, Masonic Lodge, Knights of Pythias, Salvation Army, St. Mark's Church parish, YMCA, YWCA, Woodmen Hall, Foresters of America, Independent Order of Odd Fellows (IOOF), Catholic Relief Fund, Ladies Protective Relief, and the skating rink on Addison Street were among other entities that offered assistance. Donations streamed in to the Relief Committee, among them $10,000 from the Chinese of the United States and $2,000 from the John D. Rockefeller Relief Fund.

The Native Sons of the Golden West opened their hall at 2108 Shattuck to three hundred people needing a place to sleep the night of April 19 and served

A typical resident of Tin Can Town.

GENEROSITY BY THE RAILCAR-LOAD

Berkeley relief workers were faced with the challenge of feeding thousands of refugees. Because San Francisco was the distribution hub for the entire Bay Area, the destruction of the city's warehouse district made the procurement of large quantities of food difficult. Supplies initially came from local merchants and businesses. Within a week, the YMCA on Shattuck Avenue near Allston Way was receiving food by the railcar-load. From there, supplies were transferred to the nearby headquarters of the Relief Committee.

The city of Reno sent sandwiches, home-cooked dishes, and large quantities of boiled meats, ham, and eggs. King County in Washington delivered dried fruits and canned goods. On April 23 alone, a ton of sandwiches, a ton of boiled potatoes, and 6,480 hard-boiled eggs were handed out to refugees in Berkeley.

Supplies were more than adequate, but help was needed in distributing them in the first week after the quake. Calls went out for people with experience in "the grocery line." These volunteers helped manage the deliveries: two train car–loads of groceries from Fresno County, a carload of flour, beans, and potatoes from Stockton, a carload of blankets and groceries from The Dalles, Oregon. About fifteen railcars of hospital supplies, clothing, meat, oranges, rolled oats, and even bananas were shipped to Berkeley from all over the country. The nation also sent 112 railcar-loads to San Francisco—including sandwiches, countless hard-boiled eggs, and 6,500 loaves of bread, as well as hospital supplies—which passed through Berkeley before rolling on to the city.

LEFT: *San Francisco had been the hub for food distribution. After the warehouse district burned, procuring large quantities of food was difficult.*

BELOW: *Railcars full of baggage, bedding, and supplies arriving in the East Bay.*

TOP LEFT: *In response to requests for bread, Berkeley's Golden Sheaf Bakery, produced 2,500 loaves in one day and sent them to the city on two horse-drawn wagons. In early May, Golden Sheaf replaced the Log Cabin Bakery as bread supplier to the Oakland Relief Committee, which also served Berkeley. The bakery, which received a pound of flour for every pound of bread produced, sent a total of 107,157 loaves to Oakland.*

TOP RIGHT: *Almost every San Francisco bakery was prohibited from using their ovens for fear of starting new fires.*

BOTTOM RIGHT: *A San Francisco breadline amidst the destruction.*

BOTTOM LEFT: *The first train with supplies for refugees arrives in San Francisco.*

The Berkeley YMCA, 2169 1/2 Shattuck Avenue (right), and the University YMCA crammed beds over every inch of their floors and provided meals to male refugees. The YWCA and St. Mark's Church, at Bancroft Way and Ellsworth Street (above), dedicated their facilities to the needs of women and children. Episcopal parishes opened their doors to all refugees seeking shelter.

The Salvation Army of Berkeley.

breakfast to them the next morning. The Native Sons were so moved by the plight of the refugees that they agreed to house them until they found other quarters. This generosity had a cost. According to secretary Frank McAllister, "Owing to our having our Hall open at the time of the quake and fire and feeding or at least serving almost 16,000 meals, our treasury has diminished until we are overdrawn in the Bank."[9] Two people formed a satellite relief station at Shattuck Avenue and Vine Street, where donations were accepted from people in the neighborhood. The station's staff put out a call for soap, clean rags, and clothes of all kinds. By the end of April, about ten thousand items of clothing had been distributed. Despite this largesse, supplies of certain articles, especially underwear, shoes, and blankets, ran low. The Relief Committee contacted the San Francisco Presidio and asked that these items be sent.

Neighborhood residents formed a South Berkeley Relief Committee at 2215 Ashby Avenue. They fed about three thousand earthquake victims found wandering in the Lorin district and offered them employment. Among the thousands were an estimated 150 families. South Berkeley churches combined forces in

one building, with the first floor used for feeding people, the second for making clothes for about three hundred children.

The church relief center tried to help an Italian woman who had found a three-month-old baby on a street in San Francisco's Russian Hill on the morning of April 19. The woman had gathered the baby in her arms, taken the ferry across the bay, and wound up at the South Berkeley center, where she told her story to the church women. After a few days, the woman left town, still caring for the baby. As fate would have it, another woman came into the center with a desperate air about her, and she poured out her plight of searching for her baby. She was told about the Italian woman and came back every day, hoping that the woman would return with her infant. To help her, the center placed newspaper ads asking for assistance.

Despite the damage to several important structures in West Berkeley, many buildings remained untouched and opened their doors to refugees. Fraternity Hall, at Fourth Street and University Avenue, was quickly set up as a temporary relief quarters, and the Westminster Presbyterian Church at 1901 Eighth Street

BERKELEY'S FRENCH QUARTER FEEDS ITS FRIENDS

Like many buildings, the Villa des Roses Restaurant at 2012 Fourth Street near University Avenue in West Berkeley's French Quarter had a badly damaged chimney after the earthquake. But that didn't stop Mrs. Maria Verges, the restaurant's owner and cook, from offering to feed refugees, many of whom were long-time customers. Sixty people stayed at the Villa des Roses until they could return home or find other accommodations. She never asked for a penny.

The refugees considered themselves lucky, for the seven-year-old establishment was regarded as one of the Bay Area's premier French restaurants. San Francisco residents and chefs had eagerly patronized the Villa des Roses, traveling to the East Bay by Southern Pacific train. Berkeleyans in the east part of town had come by buggy. The menu featured classic French fare: onion soup, pressed meats, fried frogs' legs, filet mignon, and French bread. The $1 price included red wine and café noir in little cups.

The Villa des Roses got its name because Mrs. Verges loved roses and planted fifteen thousand of them on the property. In the rainy season, flooding was common in the area as the neighborhood had no sewers. The restaurant became an island, and her son, Germain, would bring patrons to the door in a rowboat. When the water receded, the soil deposited on the property made great fertilizer for the roses.

A 1907 Berkeley ordinance outlawed all public consumption of alcohol, which seemed an insult to the French culture and brought an end to the French establishments in Berkeley. One by one, the restaurants closed, and West Berkeley's French Quarter was gone.

The Villa des Roses, circa 1898. The woman on the right is Mrs. Maria Verges. Her son Germain is in the middle of the front row wearing the stovepipe hat.

Combing wrecked buildings for valuables and souvenirs. Treasure hunters would seek out the rubble of jewelry stores.

A week after the earthquake, Berkeleyans went by train and ferry to see San Francisco; many brought their cameras. Sightseers crowded the rubble-strewn streets, as hawkers sold everything from fire photographs to hot dogs. Berkeley paperboy Harold Yost and his mother visited the ruins in early June. They walked up Market Street, which seemed quiet due to the absence of streetcars. The impact of the disaster hit them when they turned up Geary Street. "Five or six blocks up that street," Yost later remembered, "we could see everything: complete destruction desolation, blocks and blocks with nothing standing but broken walls. And silence: complete, eerie silence. The only sounds were the occasional muffled clangs of bits of torn metal swaying in the breeze."

and Bristol (now the west end of Hearst Avenue) provided a place for refugees to sleep and facilities for feeding them. Refugees crowded into other Oceanview camps, including the Villa des Roses restaurant and the Poplar Villa Café, both on Fourth Street.

At a morning meeting on April 20, the Relief Committee made a decision to pay the churches and other local organizations for expenses incurred housing and feeding refugees. But by 8 p.m. that night, the committee had reversed its opinion. The committee members ultimately concluded that, in the interests of sanitation and economy, refugees housed in these facilities should relocate to the California Field sanitary camp on the UC campus. A week after the earthquake, refugees from all the other camps moved to campus. A couple of days later, in an effort to further consolidate operations, the men's camp at the campus baseball field was closed and the men relocated to California Field. Private organizations were then used only to distribute goods, after the buildings that

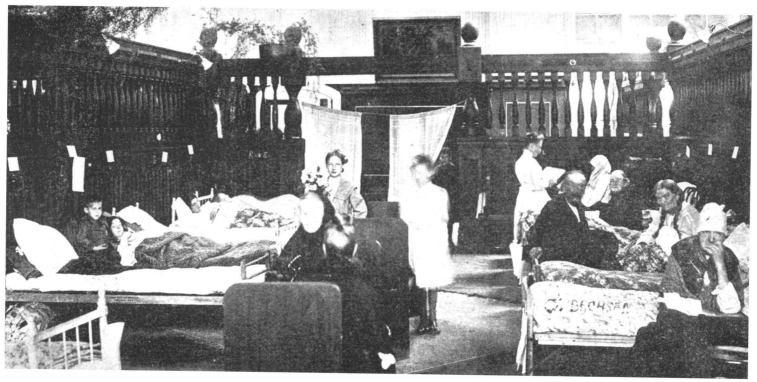

Part of the reception room of the Oakland Traction Club, which housed invalid women and children.

housed refugees were treated with disinfectants.

Tallying the number of refugees that came to Berkeley was not an easy task. The totals varied significantly from day to day as refugees came and went, moving on to other towns and being replaced by new refugees. On April 20, the Relief Committee and the *Oakland Tribune* came up with an estimate of about 10,000. By April 25, the number climbed to about 15,000, which, unlike previous estimates, included refugees outside the camps. A census taken by the Relief Committee in early May indicated that 5,000 to 6,000 refugees were still in Berkeley, 2,500 of them staying in private houses. Day by day, the number lessened, and by the end of June, the California Field camp would be closed down.[10]

The rail companies provided free passage to refugees and also to relief workers and government employees, who all wore yellow badges. By April 25, about 1,500 refugees had left Berkeley for places as far east as Ogden and as far north as Portland, seeking places to live or new employment. Passengers were

The gymnasium at the Oakland Traction Club was used as a hospital.

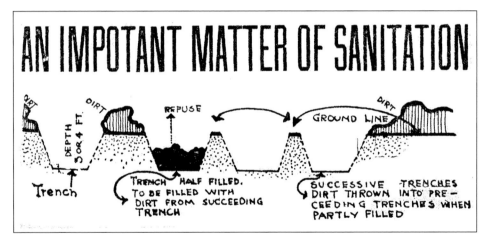

AN IMPOTANT MATTER OF SANITATION

The April 28 Oakland Tribune *printed an illustration demonstrating the proper way to construct and maintain a sanitation trench.*

carefully screened as many tramps were making use of the free transportation. Anyone of visible means was asked to pay one cent per mile for his passage during this time.[11]

Another task for relief workers was attending to the hundreds of San Franciscans in need of emergency medical treatment—people like William Cunningham, whose skull was crushed by the collapsing wall of a hotel, and C. W. Harris, a lumberman with a severely burned head, who was carried to

Berkeley. A makeshift emergency and minor surgical hospital, in addition to a hospital on the campus, was set up at the Independent Order of Odd Fellows Hall at Shattuck Avenue and Addison Street, near the Berkeley Station and the Relief Committee headquarters. The committee ran notices in the *Berkeley Gazette* instructing residents to refer the injured and ill to this hospital. Roosevelt Hospital on Dwight Way below Shattuck Avenue handled the major surgeries. During the first few weeks after the earthquake, hundreds of refugees were being cared for in Berkeley hospitals.

The fear of epidemics was almost as acute as the dread of aftershocks. A hospital for contagious diseases was quickly set up in a building at the corner of Grove and Center streets. About ten days after the quake, nine patients with contagious diseases were known to be at this isolated hospital. People afflicted with smallpox had been under quarantine in San Francisco prior to the earthquake. No one knew what happened to them afterward, but it was assumed they had fled the city. Three cases of smallpox were reportedly diagnosed in Berkeley in the first week after the earthquake. Despite the fears, there were no outbreaks of contagious illnesses.

One of the main reasons was the monitoring of the camps and the camps' refugees by people trained in sanitation techniques. Another was that the camps were hooked up to city sewers and were supplied with potable water. Chloride of lime and other disinfectants were liberally applied in the latrine trenches and wherever needed to prevent disease. Donated clothing was disinfected before use, some items so strenuously that they disintegrated. When rain started to fall heavily on April 23, wooden sidewalks were laid down in the camps and wooden floors installed in the tents, to lessen the risk of unsanitary conditions.

Mental trauma was more difficult to diagnose and treat than physical injuries and illnesses. On the night of April 23, a day before UC's baseball field camp closed, E. T. Andre of C Company, tent number six at the camp, was on patrol when he attempted to kill himself by slashing his throat. He was rushed to Roosevelt Hospital, treated, and diagnosed as suffering from temporary insanity. He was not the only one who attempted suicide that day—a number of disturbed people were carried off to the hospital, most of them protesting greatly. As the weeks wore on, the effects of the recent events continued to take their toll on the refugee population. Noting the situation, the *Oakland Enquirer* of May 18 published an interview with Dr. Adam Shirk, a well-known physician experienced in working with patients who had mental problems. "Now, in the short period of one month, since the great catastrophe," he said, "very many minds have been dethroned. Delusions of every kind have mounted the citadel of reason, illusions and hallucinations have possessed the throne of those who had not always trained themselves to the faith, that it might have been worse."

One person whose mind had been dethroned was twenty-eight-year-old Mrs. Louis Fong. She was staying at the Chinese Mission at 2504 Regent Street with her husband, the owner of a large general store in San Francisco. With their two children at their side, the couple had fought their way through the panicked crowds escaping the fire. At one moment during the pandemonium, they looked around to find their children were gone. By April 28, Mrs. Fong could no longer bear the stress of not knowing what happened to them. She grabbed a knife from the mission's kitchen table and began to chase her husband. Everyone fled the building and left her alone inside until the police arrived. Upon entering, they found Mrs. Fong calm and offering no resistance. She was gently escorted to the jail and then to a hospital in Oakland by carriage.[12]

On April 20, Mark Twain addressed a sizable crowd in New York's Carnegie Hall. After concluding his presentation, he slowly walked back to the center of the stage and said, "Let me add this final word. I offer an appeal in behalf of that multitude of that pathetic army of fathers and mothers and children, sheltered and happy two days ago now wandering hopeless, forlorn and homeless—victims of immeasurable disaster—I say I beg of you in your heart and with your purses to remember San Francisco, the smitten City."

People devised impromptu methods of contacting each other. This fence in San Francisco became a message board.

Chapter Seven

Finding Loved Ones

In 1906, when telephones were still a novelty, the telegraph was the primary method of immediate communication. But newspapers were still the reliable and most popular way to disseminate news. They often printed letters sent to residents by out-of-towners who described events in their local communities. It could take weeks for news to be published, even from a neighboring county.

After the earthquake, communication almost came to a halt. Telegraph poles and wires had collapsed, and the telephone cables under San Francisco Bay had been severed. Because the telephone and telegraph systems were not functioning, the bay became a huge physical barrier to communication. Once refugees crossed it, they were cut off from their neighborhoods and families, unless they could find one of the newspapers still being published.

People outside San Francisco were desperate to make contact with loved ones. It was hard for them not to imagine the worst. Some traveled across the country so they could look for loved ones. Even after they arrived, there was no easy way to locate or communicate with those they sought. Placing newspaper ads was one of few methods of initiating contact. The *Oakland Tribune* ran a large section, "ABOUT YOUR FAMILY AND FRIENDS," listing hundreds of displaced San Franciscans and where they were staying. The *Berkeley Daily Gazette* of April 25 ran five pages listing the latest refugees arriving in Berkeley as well as the names of people sought by frantic family and friends.

On April 25, trains finally delivered two thousand telegrams that had been delayed in their arrival to Berkeley addresses. "Alive and well. Everything lost." That was the theme of most messages. Telegraph companies offered their services

The 315-foot-tall building of the San Francisco Call *newspaper, also known as the Claus Spreckels building, at Third and Market streets, as it caught fire on April 18, 1906. A nearby fire was drawn up the elevation shaft, igniting the top floors. The steel-frame structure survived the earthquake, but its interior was gutted.*

ABOVE: *Telegraph wires were downed all over San Francisco and much of the East Bay.*

RIGHT: *A bread distribution station.*

for free. "Penniless, yet thoughtful and almost happy," the *Oakland Tribune* reported, "the throng of homeless ones have stood for hours, each patiently waiting his turn to relieve the anxiety of a distant friend or relative."[1] The companies did, however, mark the telegrams "collect" in case the recipient wished to pay.

People invented creative methods to transmit messages from San Francisco to the East Bay. General Funston sent a large quantity of bread that had arrived in San Francisco to refugees arriving in Berkeley. The loaves were delivered to the IOOF Hall on Shattuck Avenue, but some got wet, probably in the April 23 downpour, and were deemed unfit for human consumption. The spoiled loaves were given to Mrs. F. E. Daizell of 1808 Grove Street to feed to her chickens. When she cut into the loaves, she discovered that each contained a note inserted in an imperceptible slit in the bread. The notes were written in ink on fine stationery, with very good penmanship. One read as follows:

I pray you will do all you can to find May and Alphonse Saubiron of 323 Jessie st., San Francisco. He was a florist for Frank & Parodi Co., 109 Geary st., is dark, age 27, and French. Has 3 gold teeth in front of

Mouth. May is fair, age 25. Please telegram at once if you find them. I will pay for same. If they are among pay for same. See if they are among dead or injured. From an anxious sister.
Mrs. Harry Jullan Lents,
Mult. Co., Oregon.
God help you all.[2]

San Franciscans frantically tried to find friends and family in the East Bay. One man was desperate to find his sweetheart. Jew Sing, a DuPont Street merchant, had hoped to marry Ng Quei Sem on April 18. On that day, instead of getting married, he was intent on getting Ng to safety in the East Bay. He fought the San Francisco crowds to help Ng reach the San Francisco Ferry Building. As Ng's ferry pulled out of the dock, Jew could not even see her among the passengers crowded onto the ship's deck. As the ferry pulled away, Jew grew despondent. He could not bear the separation.

Jew lost everything in the destruction of Chinatown save his most valuable possessions, which he had stuffed into a bag. Within a day or two, he was able to reach Oakland, but did not know how to find Ng in the unfamiliar territory of the East Bay, now occupied by tens of thousands of refugees. Jew sought out a friend who worked in an Oakland laundry and was admired for his detective skills. Amazingly, his friend located Ng in a Berkeley refugee camp. When told of her whereabouts, Jew rushed to the camp, where he finally spotted her crying convulsively, her face buried in her hands. He ran up to her and wrapped her in his arms. Her muffled sobs slowly turned to sighs of relief. That evening, Berkeley Justice of the Peace J. P. Edgar married them. As soon as they could book passage, they left on a train for New York and a new life.[3]

Just a week after the earthquake, refugees and Berkeley townsfolk were marrying in greater and greater numbers, as were San Francisco residents. "Considering all the flirtation and lovemaking that the open air life in the parks and on the curbstones gave rise to," the October 1906 *Sunset* magazine reflected, "it is really a wonder that there were not even more of these celebrated earthquake weddings, of which we heard so much."[4]

Berkeley police marshal August Vollmer.

Chapter Eight
LAW AND ORDER

*P*roviding food and shelter was at the forefront of everyone's minds, but Berkeleyans were also concerned about criminals and con men trying to take advantage of the disruption. Berkeley police marshal August Vollmer had been on the job exactly a year and a week when the earthquake struck. He was painfully aware that his small band of policemen was no match for the thousands flooding into town. By the fourth day after the quake, citizens of Berkeley, led by UC English professor Charles Mills Gayley, petitioned Governor George Pardee to institute martial law in Berkeley. The governor refused, insisting that the civil authorities should be able to "take care of their own affairs."[1]

LEFT: *UC English professor Charles Mills Gayley.*
RIGHT: *California governor George Pardee.*

Vollmer set up six special police districts, most of them headquartered in real estate offices in the neighborhoods. He then asked for volunteers to help deal with the "large number of questionable characters" showing up in Berkeley. As many as a thousand citizens answered the call and worked largely in pairs on night patrols, from 8 p.m. to 6 a.m., to prevent fires and crime around town and in the camps. They were told to patrol "wherever there was straw," referring to the straw used in the camps to make sleeping on the ground more comfortable. UC cadets who had not gone to San Francisco were summoned for guard duty, as were their comrades when they returned from the city. Hundreds of US Army veterans were deputized. UC president Wheeler wrote to President Roosevelt that "splendid order prevails" in Berkeley only because "stringent measures" were employed.[2]

Parents were advised to keep children inside, a 10 p.m. curfew was imposed,

VETERANS RETURN TO DUTY

With the influx of thousands of refugees and the governor's refusal to instigate martial law, acting mayor Francis Ferrier and police marshal August Vollmer were forced to come up with innovative ways to maintain order. The town's police force of about a dozen men would not be nearly enough to do the job, so on April 20, the two Berkeley officials deputized hundreds of men to begin patrolling the streets.

Among them were veterans of the Civil War and the Spanish-American War armed with Springfield rifles. Some residents feared that they would be too quick to fire their weapons. One of Vollmer's captains tried to allay their fears. "My men are Civil War veterans," Captain Garlock said, "and made their reputations forty years ago and are seeking no secondhand honors by shooting at unoffending persons. They are gentlemen and treat all citizens with respect. All orders of Marshal Vollmer will be strictly obeyed. I trust the people of Berkeley will have no reason to complain of the Vets."

Captain Garlock, who commanded A Company of the Veteran Reserve, was very particular about the neatness of his camp, especially the tents and cots. One veteran was admonished because his blankets were not evenly tucked in. He replied that "if his wife visited camp and found him an experienced bedmaker she might detail him for that duty on his return home." This man was Civil War veteran John E. Boyd, called

Civil War veterans on duty at UC by the outdoor kitchen near Douglas Tilden's football statue. Among them are John E. Boyd (eleventh from left, with walrus moustache), William Henry Wiseman (third from the right, with apron), and Joseph Horner (seventh from the left, with white beard). William Wharff, an architect and builder (fourteenth from the left), had seen Abraham Lincoln on March 26, 1865, as the president rode with the troops on their way to liberate Richmond.

the "Boss Baggage Buster of Berkeley," known widely for his biting wit.

Admiring Berkeley women kept asking for souvenir cartridges from the veterans. Some of the men's cartridge belts were almost empty as a result, and Captain Garlock asked the women to refrain from such requests.

The veterans performed an indispensable service. Although all of the Civil War veterans were over sixty-five, their sense of discipline and duty was still strong. The veterans of the Spanish-American War were young men who had recently returned home. Marshal Vollmer, also a veteran of that war, had served with distinction in the Philippines.

Civil War veteran William Henry Wiseman and his wife, Margaret, at their home, 1825 Vine Street, celebrating a holiday.

Veterans of the Spanish-American War. Filipino children were posed to show the soldiers liberating them. August Vollmer, soon to become marshal of the Berkeley police force, is in the upper right.

LOAFERS MUST LEAVE BERKELEY

The following order has been placarded about the streets of this city to rid the town of men refusing to work when called upon:

"All able bodied men refusing to work on request of proper authorities must leave town.

Order of MAYOR.
Approved by Berkeley Relief Committee.

Berkeley Daily Gazette, *April 26, 1906.*

and if an able-bodied male in the camps refused work or carried a weapon, he was told to leave town. Many men departed rather than perform forced labor. Vollmer stationed officers at train stations and ferry terminals to check incoming refugees and prevent known criminals from slipping into town. Hundreds of criminals and ex-convicts were deported before they had a chance to cause trouble. Officers also patrolled the relief camps looking for pickpockets and other thieves.

As in any disaster, some people were determined to help themselves to a large serving from the public pot. To prevent undeserving people from receiving relief food, plans were made to deliver each order and have an inspector make sure the recipients were truly in need. One person caught absconding with relief supplies was Honora Bentley of 2429 Ninth Street, a wealthy Berkeley woman in her sixties with property and cash assets valued at more $60,000. Vollmer spotted her at the YMCA posing as a refugee under the alias of Mary Smith and taking food and clothing intended for San Francisco refugees. He arrested her himself. Although she could easily have posted the $1,000 bail, she let Vollmer escort her to the county jail. The story of her incarceration made front-page headlines.[3]

Stealing relief supplies became a persistent problem. At one point, Vollmer asked that several apprehended thieves be brought into his office. When the detainees entered, he acted angrier than he actually was. He told them that stealing relief supplies could be summed up in one word—*looting.* "For that there is only one penalty," he declared. He turned his head away from the men and winked at a deputy on one side of the room, then whipped his head forward and shouted, "Death!" Scowling, he told the deputies to take them away. Word of Vollmer's threat spread, and the stealing of supplies came to a halt.[4]

Vollmer was also asked to investigate rumors of local grocers selling government relief food. The government's practice was to trade its extra sugar and crackers for local grocers' stocks of soap and rice, which were in short supply in government stocks. He was unable to find grocers who illegally possessed government goods, but did admonish storeowners to keep their prices reasonable. Lorin district residents, responding to complaints of "extortionate prices," met and formed their own committee of forty-seven members to deal with the problem. One law enacted in Berkeley after the earthquake penalized merchants and express-wagon men who overcharged customers or refused to remain open for business. The penalty for violators was confiscation of the store or wagon, which was then given to someone who could run the business responsibly.

Despite the heavy rain that fell on April 23, six fires started in Berkeley, caused by fireplaces or stove flues with damaged chimneys. The next day, the city dispatched twenty-five chimney inspectors throughout the town, led by building inspector R. P. Bull. He issued an order prohibiting the use of fireplaces until the chimneys could be certified as safe by one of his men. To check a chimney, the inspector plugged the top and lit a slow-burning material such as straw in the fireplace. If a chimney was damaged, smoke could be seen leaking out the cracks. Complaints were filed about some of the specially appointed inspectors charging too much for repairs or not being qualified. Inspector Bull vowed to deal harshly with any perpetrator.

Some residents who attempted to have their chimneys repaired believed unscrupulous contractors swindled them. About twelve chimney contractors worked Berkeley at the time. One, F. S. Page and Company, was charged with asking exorbitant prices on a number of Berkeley jobs. The bricklayers and hod carriers demanded a wage increase from $4–$6 per day to $8–$10 a day. They argued that demolishing unstable, damaged brick chimneys, which were usually on the verge of collapse, was dangerous work. Inspector Bull publicly announced that he would not approve any mason's bill that "charged beyond the regular wage."[5] Even local trade councils condemned the practice of increasing wages during such an emergency.

With all the publicity given to chimney inspections, con men figured out that posing as an inspector would be an easy way to survey the valuables inside homes. A pair of men pretending to be fire chief James Kenney and building inspector Bull charmed housewives into allowing them to inspect their chimneys. The police were asked to investigate.

As both Berkeleyans and refugees began to adjust, many wished they could escape at night to the West Berkeley saloons, which had been ordered to close early, at 8 p.m., starting the evening after the earthquake. In May, with Vollmer trying to keep order and prevent criminal activities, frustrated workingmen

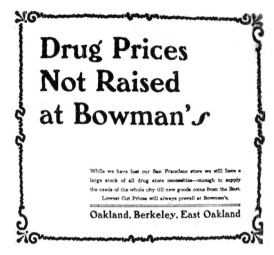

Oakland Tribune, *April 20, 1906.*

CHIMNEYS REPAIRED
AT ORDINARY PRICES

J. D. PRENTICE & SON

Room 11 Town Hall   Phone Berkeley 1209

Berkeley Daily Gazette, *April 26, 1906.*

Interior of the Stedge Saloon, near Berkeley. The early town of Stedge straddled what are now the cities of El Cerrito and Richmond.

clamored for allowing the saloons to remain open late. Others, however, spoke out just as loudly advocating that the saloons be closed entirely. The initial request to restrict the saloon hours to 7 a.m. to 8 p.m. had been made by the San Francisco Relief Council.

At a May 26 meeting of the Berkeley Board of Trustees (the city council), the trustees were presented with a petition to close the West Berkeley saloons, signed by 170 people. The same issue was on the agenda of Oakland's city council. Some Berkleyans believed that it would be useless for the city to close its saloons if Oakland did not do the same. Marshal Vollmer told the trustees that he had not noticed an increase in arrests for drunkenness and did not see that San Francisco men came to Berkeley to drink. He assured the trustees that the restricted hours were being enforced. One trustee moved that the saloons be closed until those in San Francisco reopened. The motion carried, but was overturned within weeks, when attorneys representing the saloon keepers threatened action. Everyone realized that the Oakland saloons were open for business anyway.

A pen-and-ink illustration in the May 5, 1906 Oakland Tribune *depicted the hawking of earthquake souvenirs in San Francisco.*

STRAWBERRY CREEK
UNIVERSITY OF CALIFORNIA.
BERKELEY.
PUBL.BY
ASSOCIATED
STUDENTS' STORE.

Berkeley relief officials made sure Strawberry Creek remained clean and free from garbage and soap, especially where it passed the large sanitary camps on the UC campus. They also sent out armed patrols to make sure no one drank from the creek (potable water had been piped into the camps). These measures and others helped insure the health of the refugees.

Chapter Nine

THE MILITARY TAKES CONTROL

*A*lthough Berkeley residents organized the initial relief efforts, the US Army had been a presence in town since the earthquake, largely as a visual deterrence to crime and looting. On April 28, however, the military took control of all the East Bay relief supplies and the running of the camps in Berkeley, Oakland, and Alameda. Army officials arranged a one-year lease on two Berkeley residences —at the southeast corner of Haste and Milvia streets and at 2400 Channing Way at Milvia—to serve as headquarters. The army's intent was to find a long-term solution to the refugee problem.

In the East Bay camps, refugees were put to work. One of the supervised tasks was carrying the rubbish from the camps to maintain sanitary conditions.

With the military's involvement came the enforcement of many new rules and procedures. Sanitary officers, who were in charge of proper disposal of garbage and human waste, were required to systematize the operation of the camps. A medical inspection card certifying a refugee's health was now required to enter the baths, which would be open on a limited schedule. The card also had to be shown if a refugee wanted to take shelter from the rain in Harmon Gym. A patient sent from Hearst Hall's medical facility to another hospital had to be accompanied by an armed guard, and if a guard was unavailable, the patient would be detained until one arrived. The rule was undoubtedly intended to prevent a patient with a contagious disease from infecting the public. Guards began patrolling the creeks to make sure people were not drinking the water, throwing garbage in it, or washing anything in it.

The new rules were posted in the camps: All entering had to present passes or official badges. Refugees could not leave between 9 p.m. and 6:30 a.m. Food could be brought in only with the permission of the Camp Committee. No

East Bay refugees peeling potatoes.

A refugee family in a government tent awaiting a meal.

Major James B. Erwin (seated second from right) of the Ninth Cavalry, US Army, took control of the East Bay relief effort in the first week of May.

liquor was allowed. No baggage could be removed from a camp without permission. The list went on and on. The intent was to ensure the health and safety of refugees, but to some, the enforcement of the rules felt like an inhospitable intrusion.

Around April 28, the date of the army's takeover of the camps, a big exodus of refugees took place at the UC campus. By nightfall on April 28, fewer than one hundred refugees were registered in the UC camp. Authorities expected the population of refugees throughout Berkeley to diminish as people found housing or jobs. On May 2, the *Oakland Tribune* reported that five thousand refugees remained in town, many of them in small enclaves.

The first week in May, the US War Department sent Major James B. Erwin of the Ninth Cavalry to take command of the East Bay relief effort. Major Erwin had been ordered to exert strict control over the dispersion of supplies and to relieve the various civilian relief committees. One of his first goals was to consolidate the Berkeley, Oakland, and Alameda camps at one location in Oakland called Adams Point, by Lake Merritt, near Grand Avenue. He was informed that Berkeley had been handling its own relief efforts very competently. Nevertheless, the military believed the city would welcome more experienced supervision. He

ABOVE: *An outdoor washroom at Adams Point.*

RIGHT: *The main refugee camp in Oakland, at Adams Point, where all the East Bay camps were consolidated at the end of the relief effort in June. Rows of tents can be seen in the distance in the middle of the photo.*

did encounter some resistance to his consolidation plan. "Particularly in Berkeley," Major Erwin noted, "I found an opposition that was quite strong against any effort of concentration into our camp at Adams Point."[1]

The day after Erwin took command, he inspected the Berkeley camps and found them to be in good condition. He spoke with both the people in charge and the refugees and made an effort to find out each camp's specific needs. On subsequent daily visits to the camps, he checked the conditions and pursued every complaint. He noted that only the refugees who were in "absolute need" were being admitted in the Berkeley camps and was so impressed with the policy that able-bodied men who refused to work were told to leave town that he intended to instigate it in the Oakland and Alameda camps. The policy had a clear goal. "We must do everything to induce people to return to normal life," UC president Wheeler said, "to get on their own feet . . . and support themselves."[2] Many professors had been military men, and the policies enforced at the UC camps reflected their military training.

Although Erwin felt that the town's relief committees had been quickly and competently organized, he regarded their efforts as effective strictly for

Many refugees returned to San Francisco by ferry, as illustrated in the May 1, 1906 Oakland Tribune.

emergency, short-term relief. He thought that the committees were able to perform as well as they did only because of the tremendous outpouring of support and supplies. In his opinion, the offerings of food and clothing were "lavish" and constituted a "boundless hospitality to the unfortunates of a sister city," yet "the real objects from which the Relief Committee was formed were lost sight of."[3] Erwin held the belief that support for the refugees should be efficient, prompt, and wholesome, but without luxuries, and that assistance should be provided only after each person had been screened as deserving of aid.

Erwin envisioned an efficient operation that maintained a systematic and detailed record of all supplies received and distributed. Volunteer labor had to be replaced with paid labor, so workers would be willing to take directions from an authority. Erwin thought that giving supplies to numerous fraternal organizations and churches was not a good idea, as it led to duplication of efforts. He also objected that the majority of entities that received supplies never kept records, and he claimed that the theft of supplies was rampant. The refugees, though meriting immediate assistance, should not be encouraged to rely indefinitely on government aid but should be rehabilitated as soon as possible. With this philosophy in mind, his system was instigated in all the camps in the East Bay.

Refugees receiving assistance were now required to register at the place where they received aid. They were then issued a registration card containing information about the recipient, his family, and what would be needed to put them on their feet. The card was examined by an inspector and the information reported to relief officials. Each card was scrutinized by Major Erwin and, if

Streetcars were full of refugees who rode for free after the earthquake, courtesy of the rail lines. This car traveled the Twelfth Street line in Oakland.

deemed satisfactory, was filed, and the applicant was handed a ration ticket, good for five meals. Children were allotted half-sized rations. Only one ration ticket was issued at a time, so each refugee had to be reevaluated in person when seeking a new ticket. Exceptions were made for people who could not travel. If applicants were not making sufficient efforts to establish themselves, they were pressured to find, or provided with, a job. If they refused without a good reason, their rations were not renewed. Changes were made slowly to protect women and children from suffering if their husbands or fathers failed to follow the new policies. The frequency of rations was gradually reduced to three days per week, forcing refugees to provide for themselves on the other four days and causing a large drop in the number of people applying for aid.

What also made the Berkeley camps successful was that, beginning two days after the earthquake, Mr. H. Cromarty, who chaired the Employment Committee, procured jobs for more than ten thousand men and women in Berkeley, Oakland, and Alameda. The committee tried novel approaches such as advertising particular types of jobs that might need to be filled, such as female domestic help, and arranging for potential employers to come to the committee's office to meet and immediately hire job seekers.

Erwin was also impressed with the Registration Bureau, which had made

On June 30, the steamer Caroline *transported San Francisco refugees back home from the East Bay.*

detailed records of each refugee in the camps. The records proved invaluable when friends and family sought out loved ones. Erwin kept this committee intact for the duration of the relief effort.

On May 10, the Second Squadron of the First Cavalry reported to Erwin and was assigned to guard duty in Berkeley and other East Bay towns. The squadron's job was to protect stores of supplies and supply lines and also to replace some civilian workers at the relief stations. The cavalry's I Troop was dispatched to Berkeley. The soldiers never had to use force, and the few arrests made in subsequent weeks were handled by local police officers. Berkeley residents later expressed their appreciation of the soldiers.

At the end of June, the Relief Committee of San Francisco informed Erwin that conditions had improved in the city and refugees could return. The steamer *Caroline* was leased to transport them from the East Bay to San Francisco. Each refugee or family was provided with a government tent, and the refugees and their belongings were taken to the Franklin Street Pier in Oakland. By June 30, the few refugees still residing in the Berkeley camps were given the choice of going to San Francisco or receiving one last supply of rations. To obtain aid after June 30, the remaining refugees had to go to the permanent camp in Oakland at Adams Point. Special arrangements were made to provide for elderly refugees unable to relocate. The relief committees in Berkeley agreed to move their operations to Adams Point, and the Berkeley camps were dismantled.

The Barker Block building in December of 1906 after repairs were completed.

Chapter Ten

RECOVERING AND REBUILDING

*T*he damage in the East Bay was minor compared with the devastation in San Francisco, but Berkeley still faced considerable repair work. Because school buildings had been hard-hit, the city of Berkeley began reviewing plans for the retrofitting of the surviving schools, in the hope that the structures could be seismically strengthened. Because the earthquake had occurred before the start of the school day, buildings had been empty, sparing students and teachers from serious harm. The next earthquake, it was feared, might well occur when classrooms were filled with children and teachers. At city hall, a contractor shored up the trustees' meeting room and reconstructed the damaged back wall. As soon as officials could meet, they launched an overhaul of the city's building codes.

At the Barker Block building at Shattuck Avenue and Dwight Way—which had been completed just before the earthquake—the damaged cornices, awnings, and interiors were repaired under the watchful eye of building owner J. L. Barker. The offices and apartments inside were then ready for tenants, especially displaced San Francisco businesses. On April 25, one week after the quake, the Methodist Book Concern, having lost its quarters in the city, made arrangements with Barker to move into his building. The upstairs apartments rented at a premium as refugees searched for any available housing in Berkeley.

A number of firms headed for the north end of Berkeley. Bay City Press, formerly at 628 Montgomery Street in San Francisco, opened up on Vine Street. Margret Gough moved the Gough Grocery from 871 Harrison Street in the city to 1408 Shattuck Avenue, and the Hatanaka brothers opened Tokio Laundry at 1448 Shattuck. Other businesses were attracted to West Berkeley,

Berkeley proudly advertised its growth statistics between December of 1905 and December 1906.

SARAH BERNHARDT PERFORMS

On April 26, Sarah Bernhardt gave a performance in a huge tent in Chicago to benefit the San Francisco relief effort. It was a huge success. The next month she came to California and appeared at Ye Liberty Playhouse in Oakland. Then, on May 17, she starred in the play *Phèdre* at UC Berkeley's Greek Theatre. Admission was $1 or $2 for reserved seats, and 10 percent of the proceeds went to benefit the refugees. By the time the curtain rose at 3 p.m., an audience of five thousand packed the theater. They were ready for a respite from the events of the previous month.

Bernhardt had expressed an interest in performing at the Greek Theatre after reading about it. "It has always been a dream of mine to play *Phèdre* sometime in the open air," she told the *Oakland Enquirer*. According to one review, "Her *Phèdre*, though a tragic figure in a tragedy-haunted community, supplied the first big breathing spell that the fire-sufferers had enjoyed." Bernhardt's voice "cooed and soothed and sobbed through the lines . . . and as she left the amphitheater in an open carriage without a veil, she was cheered enthusiastically by thousands of people who had lingered on the heights among the trees, or along the campus to wave and shout her an enthusiastic farewell."

Bernhardt later said, "There in the Greek Theatre of the University of California at Berkeley I played Phèdre, as it has never been played before, under blue skies and in a classic theatre of the Greek type. There sat before me eight thousand folk, of whom more than half had been made homeless by the terrible fire of San Francisco, and they forgot—yes, I believe they forgot all."

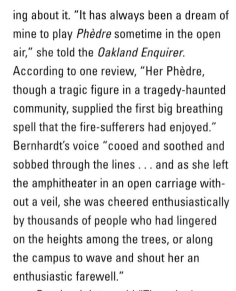

Top: *Sarah Bernhardt.*

Left: *Sarah Bernhardt in* Phèdre.

The actual program handed out at the May 17, 1906 performance of Phèdre by Sarah Bernhardt at the Greek Theatre at UC Berkeley.

ABOVE: Sarah Bernhardt gave a benefit performance for San Francisco earthquake victims in Chicago on April 26, 1906, before coming to Oakland and Berkeley, where she also donated proceeds from her performances to the relief efforts.

RIGHT: Sarah Bernhardt performed at the Ye Liberty Playhouse in Oakland in early May. San Francisco's theater district lay in ruins.

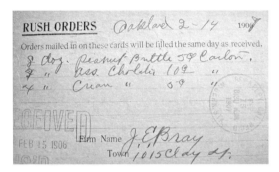

*An order sent to the Ramona Candy Company's new
Berkeley location on February 4, 1907.*

FACTORY SITES
—NEAR—
Bay Shore and Railways
WE HAVE THE GOODS
The following is a Partial List. We have others:

$450—60x100 feet.
$750—Double frontage, 44—66x250
$1250—Double frontage, 70—75x260
$1750—Corner, 120x275
$1850—Corner, 90x125
$4000—Corner, 70—115x275
$9750—Double frontage, 290x260
$11500—Three frontages, 240—285x350
$25000—Two full blocks of ground

THE ALLEN CO.   2123 Center Street

Berkeley Daily Gazette, *May 5, 1906.*

especially to the plentiful and free supply of freshwater from wells and springs. The Ramona Candy Company, once at 203 Battery Street in San Francisco, built a factory at Third and Addison streets. The company looked forward to using the local water, with its "particular purity," in the manufacture of its sweets.

Some San Francisco businessmen feared that the city would be a long time in rebuilding and believed that Berkeley offered many advantages and opportunities, the most immediate being very reasonable real estate prices. The town had established industries and a university. Transportation in the East Bay, especially the streetcars and trains, and the numerous bayside wharves were first-class. Berkeley had already been enjoying a growth spurt, and because of the earthquake, the expansion promised to continue at a heightened pace. It did not take long for this promise to become reality.

After the earthquake, the city of Berkeley quickly floated a bond measure to pay for a new municipal deepwater wharf at the end of University Avenue, which was completed in 1908. The Santa Fe and Southern Pacific railroads installed spur lines to individual industrial sites in the flatlands and West Berkeley so raw materials could be delivered directly to businesses and finished products could be shipped efficiently to customers. The Sante Fe Railroad, for example, ran spur lines to Foss Lumber and Sperry Flour. Southern Pacific ran one between Grayson and Parker streets to McCauley Co. at the waterfront.

In promotions a year prior to the earthquake, Berkeley had proudly advertised itself as "A City of Homes," a reference to the charming wood-frame residences and gardens clustered in enclaves along the town's roads. Drawn to Berkeley's alluring combination of residential neighborhoods surrounded by open spaces, hundreds of displaced San Franciscans flooded real estate offices looking for residences, as well as vacant land. Some were rich San Franciscans, as the fires had destroyed the neighborhoods of the prosperous and poor alike. Many had healthy bank accounts thanks to settlements with their insurance companies. Mason-McDuffie Real Estate dispatched a crew of twelve to find rentals to meet the need for housing. Efforts were made to keep prices reasonable in order to persuade San Francisco refugees to relocate to Berkeley. Yet, due to the demand, preventing commercial buildings from being bid up extravagantly was difficult. Some businesses simply bought residences and converted them for

The developing West Berkeley industrial area just east of the waterfront and north of Ashby, circa 1906. The Byron Jackson Iron Works can be seen on the far left.

ABOVE: *A group photo of the construction crew that built the Claremont Hotel. Construction of the hotel was begun before the earthquake and continued for years after the shaking stopped. There are stories of a new underground spring appearing on the grounds right after the earthquake.*

LEFT: *The crew at Foss Lumber Company. Their yard occupied an entire square block between Center and Addison, Milvia and Grove.*

HOUSES WANTED

Furnished and unfurnished.
We have opened a renting department temporarily.
List your houses with us at once the demand won't last.

FOR SALE
FACTORY AND WAREHOUSE SITES

Business and Residence Property,
Improved and Unimproved.

ABOVE: *Professors at UC Berkeley developed ways to recycle the tens of thousands of bricks littering San Francisco.*

LEFT: *Berkeley Daily Gazette, April 27, 1906.*

GRADUATION DAY, 1906

Benjamin Ide Wheeler, president of UC Berkeley.

On April 28, president Benjamin Ide Wheeler announced that because students and faculty had been helping with the relief effort, final exams would be canceled, and students' final grades would be based on their work during the spring term. The seniors may not have mourned the cancellation of exams, but they missed some of the pleasures routinely enjoyed by graduating classes. One of them was a yearbook. The 1906 *Blue and Gold* was about to be printed at Sunset Press in

RIGHT: *Graduation ceremonies at the Greek Theatre.*

San Francisco when the earthquake struck. The yearbook burned along with the press's other publications in the fire.

Graduation ceremonies for more than four hundred seniors took place at the Greek Theatre on May 16. President Wheeler delivered a stirring address that acknowledged recent events: "Class of 1906, I give you my blessing and send you forth. You will never forget these days of vehemence through which you issue into life. It may be you have learned more in them concerning the things that are real than in all your college course. You have learned the exceeding blessedness of helping others, you women who toiled devotedly in relief and care, and men who faithfully through hours of horror guarded the doors of the unprotected. You saw the things that men counted the real stay and foundation of life vanish to the winds; even the crust of mother earth was no longer firm beneath her feet; but out of the ruin and dismay you saw emerge a surer foundation shapen in the mind of the Eternal Real, and there composed is not land or gold or steel, but the blessed loyalties of human brotherhood and the tender mercies of human love."

Berkeley Daily Gazette, *April 26, 1906.*

commercial use.

The competition was sometimes fierce. One striking example was the Hulbert Block at Shattuck Avenue and Allston Way. Successful businessman John Hinkel, who had christened the property with his wife's maiden name, owned the block. After the earthquake, well-known developer John Havens offered Hinkel $20,000 for the block. When Hinkel did not immediately accept, Havens countered with $25,000. Hinkel's lukewarm reception to the higher sum only whetted Havens's appetite for the property. Havens upped his offer five-fold to $125,000, and Hinkel accepted. It was said that ten days after receiving the fortune Hinkel lost it in the stock market.[1]

The city struggled to keep up with the numerous building permits requested for all types of structures. In just the four months following the earthquake, thirty-seven new factories were erected. Sperry Flour, a San Francisco business, constructed a huge warehouse near the Santa Fe tracks at Addison and Bonar streets. Not far away, Foss Lumber started work on an enormous new yard covering the entire block between Center and Addison, and Milvia and Grove. Byron Jackson Iron Works, another San Francisco operation, built a large plant at Fourth and Parker streets near the railroad tracks. At the north end of Oceanview, Thomas Christie and Sons, a ship anchor foundry, put up a factory at Third and Camelia streets by the rail line. Real estate men and contractors bought up land on lower University Avenue specifically to construct plants and warehouses.

Many stores and other commercial establishments including McCloud River Lumber Co., Lewin & Meyer (wholesale grocers), Paul Elder & Co. (stationers), and Central Mercantile Co.—all former San Francisco businesses—opened in Berkeley to serve the influx of new residents. Before the earthquake, Berkeleyans had done much of their shopping in Oakland and San Francisco. In the pre-1906 era, Berkeley had the lowest proportion of businesses to its population of any Bay Area city.[2] Within two weeks after the earthquake, clothing and furniture stores reported that their sales had doubled or tripled due to the thousands of refugees who relocated in Berkeley. Developers did particularly well after the earthquake, averaging a 50 to 100 percent return on their investment when they bought tracts of land, graded for roads and homesites, and sold the

Berkeley Daily Gazette, April 26, 1906.

Berkeley Daily Gazette, April 27, 1906.

Berkeley Daily Gazette, April 26, 1906.

Berkeley Daily Gazette, May 5, 1906.

Berkeley Daily Gazette, May 3, 1906.

The Sante Fe tracks crossing just south of University Avenue, seen on the right. The tower of the Hofburg Brewery on San Pablo Avenue is in the center of the photo.

ABOVE: *Berkeley Daily Gazette, April 30, 1906.*

LEFT: *On May 14, members of the Ruskin Club and their families went to the Berkeley hills for a picnic. Afterward, M. V. Holloway gave a talk, "The Earthquake and Socialism." He noted how the earthquake brought to the forefront the compassionate side of human nature. Dependency on an unreliable water source and cheap construction, he claimed, were responsible for the destruction, and the predictable result would be the consolidation of wealth in the hands of a few large operators.*

lots to eager buyers. Lots in neighborhoods formerly regarded as far away from town, such as the Elmwood, were in demand. Tracts in other outlying areas would soon be laid out, mapping the future of Berkeley and creating such neighborhoods as Cragmont, Thousand Oaks, and Northbrae, names still in use today.

Homeless San Franciscans scooped up property in north Berkeley, where the Berkeley Land Company had laid lots on six hundred acres near Spruce and Josephine streets, purchased in early 1906 for $1,450,000. For months before the earthquake, wealthy Chicagoan E. H. Harris had been eyeing a prime lot in the district of Northbrae. He finally bought it and was asked if the earthquake made him regret his move to Berkeley. "I would rather have an earthquake every morning for breakfast here," he replied, "than experience one eastern tornado."[3]

In 1900, Berkeley's population was just over thirteen thousand. In 1906, it approached twenty-six thousand. Within the year after the earthquake, the town had grown by 50 percent to thirty-eight thousand residents. From 1900 to 1910, Berkeley had the largest gain "of any city of similar rank in the country."[4]

With the burgeoning population and new housing and businesses—and the

ARRIVALS IN ALBANY

Many Italian American earthquake refugees from San Francisco relocated to the area we know as Albany, attracted to its wide-open landscape and pastureland. Some were convinced to settle there because it was an undeveloped area without tall buildings to collapse in the event of another earthquake. Entire families arrived on their new land by horse-drawn wagon. Most camped out in tents while they built their new homes. The homes were small by our standards, but satisfied the needs of families of that time when possessions were few and open spaces provided all the entertainment the children needed.

Neighbors helping newcomers was the tradition in the neighborhood. As new homes sprung up, they filled in the wide-open spaces that once separated the area's few, scattered houses. Those who could afford them had wells dug on their land, and windmills soon dotted the terrain.

The roads, like those in Berkeley, were, depending on the weather, either muddy or dusty, and catching a train was not an easy task. Nor was finding one's way home in the dark, and lanterns were commonly stored at the train stops in the morning for the return walk home at the end of the day.

Albany's first school was built in 1908, prior to which classes were held in a barn at the corner of San Pablo and Brighton avenues. Grocery and general stores appeared and a community began to grow.

ABOVE: *A small shack in Albany with its proud owner, Clarence Rhodes, and his daughter, Leona.*

LEFT: *The new home of Hans Hensen in the new city of Albany, with Mayor Frank Roberts leaning on the fence.*

JOHN SPRING'S ALBANY

In 1906, after the earthquake, the Realty Syndicate sold a tract of land by the bay to developer John Spring. Spring named his 142-acre development Regent Park. Today we know it as Albany. Compared with Berkeley, land was cheap. Lots near San Pablo Avenue sold for $800. For a down payment of just $50, the buyer could take possession.

In 1909, Spring purchased another 92 acres, just east of Regent Park and abutting the Northbrae tract. This became the Thousand Oaks tract. Spring went on to purchase some of the Northbrae tract from Mason-McDuffie.

ABOVE: *Albany in 1909.*

RIGHT: *A family in their new Albany home. Albany Hill is in the background.*

ABOVE: *A toddler looks on as the new neighborhood of Northbrae is developed.*

RIGHT: *The commercial corner of Adeline and Alcatraz in the Lorin district, circa 1910.*

post-earthquake recognition of the importance of prompt communication during emergencies—came modern utilities. What was once considered a novelty was now a necessity. The Bay Counties Power Company had already strung wires throughout Berkeley before the earthquake and began to meet the expanded demand for electricity. Kerosene lamps would soon become an artifact of a bygone era. Grounded telephone wiring was laid in the new residential tracts, and the pre-existing system was rewired. In 1900 barely seven hundred households in Berkeley had telephones. By 1911, a telephone that both made outgoing calls and received incoming calls could be found in nearly every home. The growth in transportation facilities was equally dramatic. In 1901 only one train pulled into the Berkeley Station each hour. A decade later, 112 trains, in addition to the many electric streetcars, served Berkeley daily. The population had ballooned to such an extent that postmaster George Schmidt hired six new mail carriers to relieve the backup in deliveries.

The 1906 earthquake, though a tragedy of massive proportions, transformed Berkeley with a suddenness and thoroughness that only an act of nature could orchestrate. At the turn of the century, Berkeley was a quiet university town. Following the quake, it was a city ready for the new century. Berkeleyans met the refugees with remarkable resourcefulness and compassion, and were, in turn, invigorated by the experience. For a century, people have looked to San

The Elmwood district as it was when it was put on the market for development in 1907.

Francisco to understand the calamity of the Great Earthquake of 1906, but a significant piece of the puzzle resides across the bay, having arrived with the thousands of refugees that rushed to Berkeley, changing both cities forever.

ACKNOWLEDGMENTS

I extend very special and heartfelt gratitude to three talented and dedicated professionals, Thomas A. Smart, Esq., Robert Barnes, Esq., and Victoria Haje, Esq., all of the firm Kaye Scholer LLP, whose brilliant work in the copyright field resolved crucial issues regarding my use of historical material.

In writing this book, I had invaluable help from many generous people and institutions. For providing photographs and historical information, I thank the following associates and friends:

Albany Fire Chief Marc McGinn and the Albany Fire Department; Richard Russo and the staff of the Alameda County Library, Albany Branch; Russell Schock and the University of California Alumni Association; Donald Beeson, Esq.; the Berkeley Architectural Heritage Association and Wendy Markel, Leslie Emmington, Anthony Bruce, Carrie Olson, Susan Cernie, Stephanie Manning, Austene Hall, and Janice Thomas; the University of California Bancroft Library, especially Susan Snyder, Erica Nordmeier, David Farrell, Peter Hanff, David Kessler, Dean Smith, and Iris Donovan; the Berkeley Firefighters Association and Michael Flynn (for his many acts of friendship over the years) and Randy Olsen; Tom Fortin, Jane Scantlebury, and the staff of the Berkeley Public Library History Room; South Berkeley Branch Library and Jerri Ewart, Kay Finny, and staff; Sergeant Michael J. Holland, retired, head of the Historical Preservation Society of the Berkeley Police Department; Shiela Soo and Leslie Rome of the City of Berkeley Clerks Department; Rachel Rupert and the Berkeley Chamber of Commerce; Xavier Hernandez Jr. and the staff of the *Blue and Gold Yearbook* of UC Berkeley; John Brennan, for giving me his treasured pioneer family photos and for sharing his Brennan family charm and good friendship; Builders Booksource, especially George and Sally Kiskaddon; the California State Library and Dawn L. Rodriques; the Carnegie Institution, especially Tina McDowell and John Strom; James Chanin, Esq., for the loan of his collections; Walter Crinnion, whose ancestors helped build Berkeley; Victoria Jourdan and staff at the Newspapers and Periodicals Room of the Doe Library of UC Berkeley; Barbara Gamba, for sharing her treasured family photos and for editing an earlier version of the text; Irlene M. Castagliola and *Harper's* magazine; the Hayward Area Historical Society and Dianne Curry; Erica Mailman, for help with the Joaquin Miller photo; Stephanie and Kurt Manning, for photo contributions and their decades of work in preserving West Berkeley; the *Oakland Tribune* and Theresa Martinez and Mario Dianda; the Oakland Public Library History Room and Steve Lavoie, Simone Klugman, Kathleen Di Giovanni, and Lynn Culter, for answering so many of my questions; the Oakland Public Library Newspaper and Magazine Room and Paul Schiesser, Terry Egan, George Celli, Ricardo Antoni, Siegfried Kutin, Joan Garvin, Nadina Wilson, and staff, for making my research much easier; Ellen M. Weston and the Pacific School of Religion, for sharing their history and collections; Penny Hearn Adams, for loaning me her wonderful family photos; Ginny Cain and Prudential California Realty, for happily helping me gather material; the San Francisco Public Library History Room and Greg Kelly and staff, for always offering assistance; John Waide, University Archivist, Dr. Randy R. McGuire, Assistant University Archivist, and Melanie Whittington, Saint Louis University; Jeanie Shaterian and Charles McLaughlin for sharing their father's interview; Sandra Sher, for sharing earthquake reference data and for her decades of being a friend of preservation; Rev. C. Robbins Clark and St. Mark's Church, for opening the church photos to me; Jerry Sulliger, for discussing the details of early Berkeley and for his love of Berkeley history; *Sunset* magazine and Lorraine Reno; the great pioneer Teague family: Gary and Joan Herbertson, Gail Ramsey, Beverley Hansen, and Jim Herbertson and their families; the late Madelyn "Mika" Wright, whose memories of ninety years in Berkeley will be a gift to future generations; the Western Train Museum and Bart Nadeau and Harry Aitken, for their able and extra assistance; Richard Wessel, for his untiring search for lost Berkeley history and for sharing what he finds; Sarah Wickander, for being an invaluable resource to many in the Berkeley history community; Steve Zerbe, a real professional researcher of history on many fronts.

Special mention goes to those who have helped with the production of this book: Dr. Gray Brechin, geographer and author of *Imperial San Francisco: Urban Power, Earthly Ruin,* for his willingness to put his time, large talents, and support toward my history endeavors and for writing the book's foreword;

Charles Denson, Coney Island historian and author of *Coney Island: Lost and Found,* for his ideas and support and for suggesting the title of the book; to Judith Dunham, for her professional vision in editing and guiding the book; Steve Edwards, for reading my manuscripts and offering knowledgeable suggestions; Lisa Elliot of Elysium Design, for making *Berkeley 1900* and this book the best they can be; Sue Rosenthal, for reading my manuscripts and offering valuable advice; Maggie Newsom, for reading every manuscript and offering valuable feedback; Melissa Schwarz, for reading my manuscripts and giving insightful feedback; and the employees of Copy Central at 1553 Solano Avenue who always offered such friendly help in making my copies, especially manager Greg Tomeoni, Gregg Schmalz, and Lynn McBride.

I also thank Mayor Gavin Newsom of San Francisco for being the first of the city's mayors to publicly recognize the relief efforts of the citizens of Berkeley in response to the needs of San Francisco refugees; and David Carrington Miree, Communications Officer, San Francisco Mayor's Office of Communications, and James "Jimmer" Cassiol, Office Manager, San Francisco Mayor's Office of Neighborhood Services, for issuing a Certificate of Honor to the citizens of Berkeley for their efforts.

I acknowledge and thank the Berkeley Civic Arts Program and the Civic Arts Commission for their support and grants, which have helped sustain my historical writing and preservation efforts in Berkeley. I would like to thank Mary Ann Merker and Charlotte Fredricksen for their efforts with the program.

And I would also like to acknowledge my family for their support and caring: my parents, Milton and Mildred Schwartz; my brother-in-law Tom Smart and nephews Cody and Zac; my cousins Roberta, Meredith, Dylan, and Rachael; my Aunt Blanche and Uncle Al; and my cousins Stevie, Andrea, Marcie, Candy, David, Sydney, Marlyn, Herbie, Ronnie, Marc, and Susan.

NOTES

Chapter One

1. Harold Yost, "The Day the City Trembled: An Eyewitness Remembers," *Independent and Gazette*, April 19, 1981.

Chapter Two

1. Harold Yost, "The Day the City Trembled: An Eyewitness Remembers," *Independent and Gazette*, April 19, 1981.
2. "Damage Done at Berkeley," *Oakland Tribune*, April 18, 1906.
3. Harold Yost, "The Day the City Trembled: An Eyewitness Remembers," *Independent and Gazette*, April 19, 1981.
4. George Ploughman, "Account by George Ploughman," unpublished typescript, Berkeley Architectural Heritage Association.

Chapter Three

1. Harold Yost, "The Day the City Trembled: An Eyewitness Remembers," *Independent and Gazette*, April 19, 1981.
2. "Damage Done at Berkeley," *Oakland Tribune*, April 18, 1906.
3. "Berkeley Boasts Haughty Past," Knave, *Oakland Tribune*, January 22, 1967.
4. "Berkeley Is Most Fortunate of the Cities About the Bay," *Berkeley Daily Gazette*, April 18, 1906.

Chapter Four

1. "Firemen in Panic," *Oakland Tribune*, April 19, 1906.
2. "Cadets Do Good Work," *Berkeley Daily Gazette*, April 23, 1906.
3. "U.C. Cadet Will Be Lame for Life," *Berkeley Daily Gazette*, July 1, 1906.
4. William Bronson, *The Earth Shook, The Sky Burned* (San Francisco: Chronicle Books, 1959), 60.
5. Julian Willard Helburn, "The Quickening Spirit: The San Francisco That Survived," *American Magazine*, July 1906, 295.
6. Sayre MacNeil, "Cadets in Active Service," in *1908 Blue and Gold of the University of California: The University of California Annual* (Berkeley: University of California, 1907), unpaginated.
7. Ibid.
8. "Complain of the Cadets," *Oakland Tribune*, April 22, 1906.

Chapter Five

1. Donald McLaughlin, interview by Charles C. McLaughlin, January 8, 1976, tape recording, collection of Charles C. McLaughlin and Jeanie McLaughlin Shaterian.
2. Hal Johnson, "Earthquake Aftermath," So We're Told, *Berkeley Gazette*, April 23, 1951.

3. "Chinese Editor on the Great Calamity," *Oakland Enquirer,* April 21, 1906.
4. Julian Willard Helburn, "The Quickening Spirit: The San Francisco That Survived," *American Magazine,* July 1906, 294–95.
5. Workers of the Writers' Program of the Work Projects Administration in Northern California, *Berkeley: The First Seventy-Five Years* (Berkeley: Gillick Press, 1941), 84.
6. James Grey, "How Big Quake Felt to Little Berkeley Boy," *Independent and Gazette,* April 19, 1981.
7. Alice G. Eccles, "Telegraph Wires Are Laden with Messages," *Oakland Tribune,* April 22, 1906.
8. "Message Comes to Pardee from Roosevelt," *Oakland Tribune,* April 19, 1906.

Chapter Six

1. Benjamin Ide Wheeler to Theodore Roosevelt, 23 April 1906, Benjamin Ide Wheeler Papers: circa 1870–1923, Bancroft Library, University of California, Berkeley.
2. Hal Johnson, "Earthquake Aftermath," So We're Told, *Berkeley Gazette,* April 23, 1951.
3. John Dundas Fletcher, "An Account of the Work of the Relief Organized in Berkeley in April and May, 1906, for the Refugees from San Francisco" (master's thesis, University of California, April 1909), 8–9.
4. Ibid., 16.
5. "Over 20,000 Chinese Are Now in Oakland," *Oakland Tribune,* April 22, 1906.
6. "Chinese Refugees Are Well Treated," *Oakland Tribune,* April 28, 1906.
7. James Grey, "How Big Quake Felt to Little Berkeley Boy," *Independent and Gazette,* April 19, 1981.
8. Hal Johnson, "Anniversary of a Jar," So We're Told, *Berkeley Gazette,* April 17, 1947.
9. Charles Marinovich, "The Quake: Yes, It Happened Here, Too," *Independent and Gazette,* April 26, 1981.
10. John Dundas Fletcher, "An Account of the Work of the Relief Organized in Berkeley in April and May, 1906, for the Refugees from San Francisco" (master's thesis, University of California, April 1909), 6–7.
11. Ibid., 22–23.
12. "Chinese Woman Insane," *Berkeley Daily Gazette,* April 28, 1906.

Chapter Seven

1. Alice G. Eccles, "Telegraph Wires Are Laden with Messages," *Oakland Tribune,* April 22, 1906.
2. "Notes Hidden in Loaves of Bread," *Berkeley Daily Gazette,* April 26, 1906.
3. "Romance of a Chinese Wedding," *Berkeley Daily Gazette,* April 27, 1906.
4. Edwin Emerson Jr., "San Francisco at Play," *Sunset,* October 1906, 320.

Chapter Eight

1. "Berkeley Would Have Martial Law," *Oakland Enquirer,* April 21, 1906.

2. Benjamin Ide Wheeler to Theodore Roosevelt, 23 April 1906, Benjamin Ide Wheeler Papers: circa 1870–1923, Bancroft Library, University of California, Berkeley.
3. "Wealthy Woman Tries to Defraud," *Berkeley Reporter*, April 30, 1906.
4. Alfred E. Parker, *The Berkeley Police Story* (Springfield, IL: Charles C. Thomas, 1972), 11.
5. "Bricklayers' Bills Must Be 'O. K.,'" *Oakland Tribune*, April 26, 1906.

Chapter Nine

1. Harris Bishop, ed., *Souvenir and Resume of Oakland Relief Work to San Francisco Refugees* (Oakland: Press of Oakland Tribune, 1906).
2. Benjamin Ide Wheeler to Theodore Roosevelt, 6 May 1906, Benjamin Ide Wheeler Papers: circa 1870–1923, Bancroft Library, University of California, Berkeley.
3. Harris Bishop, ed., *Souvenir and Resume of Oakland Relief Work to San Francisco Refugees* (Oakland: Press of Oakland Tribune, 1906).

Chapter Ten

1. Hal Johnson, "House of Hinkel," So We're Told, *Berkeley Daily Gazette*, August 12, 1941.
2. Warren Cheney, "Commercial Berkeley," *Sunset*, November 1906, 70.
3. "Big Demand for Property," *Berkeley Daily Gazette*, April 30, 1906.
4. Wells Drury, *Berkeley, California*, 1912.

BIBLIOGRAPHY

Alameda County Illustrated: The Eden of the Pacific. Oakland: Tribune Publishing, 1898.

Atherton, Gertrude. *Ancestors.* New York: Harper and Brothers, 1907.

Bagwell, Beth. "Idora Park Was Oakland Highlight." *The Montclairian,* July 26, 1978.

Banks, Charles Eugene. *The History of the San Francisco Disaster and Mount Vesuvius Horror.* 1906.

Berkeley Advocate, April 17, 1890.

Berkeley Architectural Heritage Association. *Thousand Oaks.* Berkeley: Berkeley Architectural Heritage Association, 1997.

Berkeley-California, A City of Homes. Berkeley: Conference Committee of the Improvement Club of Berkeley, California, 1905.

Berkeley Daily Gazette, April 3, 1903, April 17–August 30, 1906.

———, "Berkeley Is Most Fortunate of the Cities About the Bay," April 18, 1906.

———, "Big Demand for Property," April 30, 1906.

———, "Cadets Do Good Work," April 23, 1906.

———, "Chinese Woman Insane," April 28, 1906.

———, "Family of Jacobson," July 11, 1951.

———, "G.A.R. Camp on the Campus," May 1, 1906.

———, "Notes Hidden in Loaves of Bread," April 26, 1906.

———, "Romance of a Chinese Wedding," April 27, 1906.

———, "U.C. Cadet Will Be Lame for Life," July 1, 1906.

———, "Veterans Now Ready for Duty," May 5, 1906.

Berkeley Reporter, Christmas issue, December 1906.

———, "Wealthy Woman Tries to Defraud," April 30, 1906.

Bishop, Harris, ed. *Souvenir and Resume of Oakland Relief Work to San Francisco Refugees.* Oakland: Press of Oakland Tribune, 1906.

Bronson, William. *The Earth Shook, The Sky Burned.* San Francisco: Chronicle Books, 1959.

Call-Chronicle-Examiner, April 19, 1906.

The Camera Story of the San Francisco Earthquake and Fire. Los Angeles: Geo. Rice and Sons, n.d.

Carlin, Eva V. *A Berkeley Year.* Berkeley: Women's Auxiliary of the First Unitarian Church, 1898.

Cheney, Warren. "Commercial Berkeley." *Sunset* 18, no. 1 (November 1906): 70–79.

Citizens of Albany. *The Story of Albany.* Albany: Albany Police and Fire Employees Civil Service Club, 1947.

Clemens, Dorothy Thelen. *Standing Ground and Starting Point: 100 Years with the University YWCA.* Berkeley: University YWCA, 1990.

Collier's 38, no.6 (May 5, 1906), no.7 (May 12, 1906).

Dean, Sara. *Travers: A Story of the San Francisco Earthquake.* New York: Frederick A. Stokes, 1907.

Drury, Wells. *Berkeley, California.* 1912.

Eccles, Alice G. "Telegraph Wires Are Laden with Messages." *Oakland Tribune,* April 22, 1906.

Emerson, Edwin Jr. "San Francisco at Play." *Sunset* 17, no. 6 (October 1906): 319–28.

Everett, Marshall. *Complete Story of the San Francisco Earthquake.* Chicago: Bible House, 1906.

Fletcher, John Dundas. "An Account of the Work of the Relief Organized in Berkeley in April and May, 1906, for the Refugees from San Francisco." Master's thesis. University of California, Berkeley, 1909.

Forbes, Charles Noyes. Letter to Carrie Hyde Forbes, April 22, 1906. Paul and Sandra Little History Collection.

Gamba, Barbara. *Turning Point: Berkeley Clinic Auxiliary 1917–1954.* Berkeley: privately published, 2004.

Glimpses of the San Francisco Disaster. Chicago: Laird and Lee, 1906.

Grey, James. "How Big Quake Felt to Little Berkeley Boy." *Independent and Gazette*, April 19, 1981.

Hanson, Gladys, and Emmet Condon. *Denial of Disaster.* San Francisco: Cameron and Company, 1989.

Harper's Weekly 1, no. 2576 (May 5, 1906), no. 2577 (May 12, 1906), no. 2578 (May 19, 1906).

Helburn, Julian Willard. "The Quickening Spirit: The San Francisco That Survived." *American Magazine* 62, no. 3 (July 1906): 294–301.

Irwin, Will. *The City That Was.* New York: R. W. Huebsch, 1906.

———. "San Francisco a Month Ago." *Everybody's Magazine* 14, no. 6 (June 1906): 753–60.

Johnson, Hal. "Anniversary of a Jar," So We're Told. *Berkeley Gazette*, April 17,1947.

———. "Anniversary of a Jar," So We're Told. *Berkeley Gazette*, April 18,1951.

———. "Earthquake Aftermath," So We're Told. *Berkeley Gazette*, April 23,1951.

———. "House of Hinkel," So We're Told. *Berkeley Gazette,* August 12, 1941.

Jones, William Carey. *Illustrated History of the University of California.* Berkeley: Student's Cooperative Society, 1901.

Lawson, Andrew C. *The California Earthquake of April 18, 1906: Report of the State Earthquake Investigation Commission in Two Volumes and Atlas.* Washington, DC: Carnegie Institution of Washington, 1908. Reprint, 1969.

Leach, Frank A. *Recollections of a Newspaperman.* San Francisco: Samuel Levinson, 1917.

Livingstone, Alexander P. *Complete Story of San Francisco's Terrible Calamity of Earthquake and Fire.* N.p.: Continental Publishing, n.d.

MacNeil, Sayre. "Cadets in Active Service." In *1908 Blue and Gold of the University of California: The University of California Annual.* Berkeley: University of California, 1907.

Marinovich, Charles. "The Quake: Yes, It Happened Here, Too." *Independent and Gazette,* April 26, 1981.

———. "Remembering the Shock of the '06 Earthquake." *Independent and Gazette,* April 5, 1981.

McLaughlin, Donald. Interview by Charles C. McLaughlin. January 8, 1976. Tape recording.

Collection of Charles C. McLaughlin and Jeanie McLaughlin Shaterian.

Morris, Charles, ed. *The San Francisco Calamity by Earthquake and Fire*. Publisher unknown, 1906.

The New San Francisco Magazine 1, no. 1 (May 1906).

Northbrae: A Residence Park at Berkeley. Berkeley: Mason-McDuffie, n.d.

Oakland, Alameda and Berkeley Directory. Oakland: Sunset Telephone and Telegraph, August 1906.

Oakland Enquirer, April 1–June 30, 1906.

———, "Berkeley Would Have Martial Law," April 21, 1906.

———, "Chinese Editor on the Great Calamity," April 21, 1906.

Oakland Tribune, April 17–June 30, 1906.

———, "Berkeley Boasts Haughty Past," Knave, January 22, 1967.

———, "Bricklayers' Bills Must Be 'O. K.,'" April 26, 1906.

———, "Chinese Refugees Are Well Treated," April 28, 1906.

———, "Complain of the Cadets," April 22, 1906.

———, "Damage Done at Berkeley," April 18, 1906.

———, "The Eucalyptus a Disappointment," Knave, January 10, 1971.

———, "Firemen in Panic," April 19, 1906.

———, "Message Comes to Pardee from Roosevelt," April 19, 1906.

———, "Over 20,000 Chinese Are Now in Oakland," April 22, 1906.

———, "Poet Miller Tells of Great Quake and Fire," May 6, 1906.

Out West 24, no. 6 (June 1906).

Overland Monthly 47, no. 4 (April 1906), no. 5 (May 1906), no. 6 (June 1906).

Overland Monthly 48, no. 1 (July 1906), no. 2 (August 1906), no. 3 (September 1906).

Palmer, Frederick. "San Francisco in Ruins." *Collier's* 38, no. 6 (May 5, 1906): 9–28.

Parker, Alfred E. *The Berkeley Police Story*. Springfield, IL: Charles C. Thomas, 1972.

Pettitt, George A. *Berkeley: The Town and Gown of It*. Berkeley: Howell-North Books, 1973.

The Picture Story of the San Francisco Earthquake. Los Angeles: Geo. Rice and Sons, n.d.

Ploughman, George. "Account by George Ploughman." Unpublished typescript. Collection of Berkeley Architectural Heritage Association.

Ransome, Frederick Leslie. "The Probable Cause of the San Francisco Earthquake." *National Geographic* 17, no. 5 (May 1906): 280–300.

Rosen, Linda. "Spenger's Oral History Recalls 1906 Quake." *Berkeley Voice*, April 25, 1984.

San Francisco Art Institute. "History of SFAI." *Early and Founding Years*. http://www.sfai.edu/page.aspx?page=135.

San Francisco: Before and After the Great Earthquake, April 18, 1906. Los Angeles: Balloon Route, 1906.

The San Francisco Catastrophe. St. Joseph, MO: S. A. Moore, 1906.

The San Francisco Disaster Photographed. New York: C. S. Hammond, 1906.

San Francisco Earthquake Edition. Los Angeles: J. L. Le Berthon, n.d.

San Francisco: The Story of the Earthquake Told with Views of the Doomed City. Portland:

L. H. Nelson, 1906.

Scenes of the San Francisco Fire and Earthquake, Series No. 2. San Francisco: Phoenix Photo, 1906.

Searight, Frank Thompson. *The Doomed City, a Thrilling Tale*. Chicago: Laird and Lee, 1906.

Sher, Sandra. "How Do You Spell Relief? O-A-K-L-A-N-D." *The Museum of California*, March–April 1987.

Sibley, Robert, ed. *The Golden Book of California*. Berkeley: California Alumni Association, 1937.

Sign of the Times 32, no. 25 (June 27, 1906).

Stetson, James, and George Brooks. *The San Francisco Earthquake of April, 1906*. Nashville, GA: Wayne and Judy Dasher, 2003.

Sunset 17, no. 1–6 (May–October 1906).

Sunset 18, no. 1 (November 1906).

Trolley Talk 2 , no. 5 (May 1906).

Tyler, Sydney. *San Francisco's Great Disaster*. Philadelphia: P. W. Ziegler, 1906.

Virtual Museum of the City of San Francisco. "Mark Hopkins Institute of Art." *Biennial Report of the President of the University on behalf of the Regents to His Excellency the Governor of the State, 1904-1906*. http://www.sfmuseum.org/1906.2/hopkins.html.

Wallace, Janette Howard. "Reminiscences of Janette Howard Wallace." Unpublished typescript. 1986. Bancroft Library, University of California, Berkeley.

Waterman, S. D. *History of the Berkeley Schools*. Berkeley: privately published, 1918.

Wheeler, Benjamin Ide. Papers: circa 1870–1923. Bancroft Library, University of California, Berkeley.

Whitaker, Herman. "The Human Drama at San Francisco." *Harper's Weekly* 1, no. 2578 (May 19, 1906): 694–98.

White, Trumbull. *Complete Story of the San Francisco Horror*. N.p.: Hubert D. Russell, 1906.

Wilson, James Russel. *San Francisco's Horror of Earthquake and Fire*. Philadelphia: Percival Supply, 1906.

Workers of the Writers' Program of the Work Projects Administration in Northern California. *Berkeley: The First Seventy-Five Years*. Berkeley: Gillick Press, 1941.

Yost, Harold. "The Day the City Trembled: An Eyewitness Remembers." *Independent and Gazette*, April 19, 1981.

Zeigler, Wilbur Gleason. *Story of the Earthquake and Fire*. San Francisco: Leon C. Osteyee and Murdock Press, 1906.

IMAGE SOURCES

Front Matter

Page ii: Collection of Sarah Wickander.

Page vi: Berkeley Architectural Heritage Association.

Page xii: Vernon Sappers Collection, Western Railway Museum, BAERA #20208.

Chapter One

Page 1: Collection of Anthony Bruce.

Page 2: *Top,* Vernon Sappers Collection, Western Railway Museum, BAERA #24260;
    bottom, Vernon Sappers Collection, Western Railway Museum, BAERA #16378.

Page 3: *Left,* California History Room, California State Library, Sacramento, California; *right,*
    Berkeley Firefighters Association.

Page 4: *Top, 1908 Blue and Gold of the University of California; bottom,* Prudential Realty.

Page 5: *Alameda County Illustrated: The Eden of the Pacific.*

Page 6: *Left,* private collection; *right, 1908 Blue and Gold of the University of California.*

Page 7: *Berkeley Daily Gazette,* April 11, 1903.

Chapter Two

Page 8: *Out West,* June 1906.

Page 9: Collection of Teague/Herbertson family.

Page 10: Oakland History Room, Oakland Public Library.

Page 11: *Illustrated History of the University of California,* William Carey Jones.

Page 13: *Left,* Saint Louis University Archives; *right, Illustrated History of the University of
    California,* William Carey Jones.

Chapter Three

Page 14: *The New San Francisco Magazine,* May 1906.

Page 15: *Berkeley Reporter,* Christmas issue, 1906, Berkeley Firefighters Association.

Page 16: *The California Earthquake of April 18, 1906, Report of the State Earthquake
    Investigation Commission in Two Volumes and Atlas,* Andrew C. Lawson.

Page 17: *The California Earthquake of April 18, 1906: Report of the State Earthquake
    Investigation Commission in Two Volumes and Atlas,* Andrew C. Lawson.

Page 18: Berkeley History Room, Berkeley Public Library.

Page 19: *Left,* Berkeley Firefighters Association; *right,* Bancroft Library, UC Berkeley,
    1981.056:7-PIC.

Page 20: *Left, Berkeley, California,* Wells Drury; *right,* Berkeley Firefighters Association.

Page 21: *Left,* Berkeley Firefighters Association; *right, Berkeley, California,* Wells Drury.

Page 22: *Top left and bottom left,* Berkeley History Room, Berkeley Public Library; *right,*
    Berkeley Architectural Heritage Association.

Page 76: *Top left, Berkeley-California, A City of Homes; bottom left,* The Salvation Army and Captain Wright, Berkeley Corp Officer; *right,* Berkeley Firefighters Association.

Page 77: *Independent and Gazette,* April 5, 1981.

Page 78: Berkeley Firefighters Association.

Page 79: Private collection.

Page 80: *Trolley Talk,* May 1906, Western Railway Museum.

Page 81: *Top, Trolley Talk,* May 1906; *bottom, Oakland Tribune,* April 28, 1906.

Page 82: Private collection.

Page 83: *Oakland Enquirer,* May 5, 1906.

Chapter Seven

Page 84: *Complete Story of the San Francisco Horror,* Trumbull White.

Page 85: *Sunset,* June 1906.

Page 86: *Left, Complete Story of the San Francisco Earthquake,* Marshall Everett; *right, The San Francisco Catastrophe.*

Chapter Eight

Page 88: Berkeley Firefighters Association.

Page 89: *Left, Illustrated History of the University of California,* William Carey Jones; *right, Complete Story of the San Francisco Horror,* Trumbull White.

Page 90: Private collection.

Page 91: *Left,* Berkeley Firefighters Association; *right,* Collection of Gamba Family.

Page 92: *Berkeley Daily Gazette,* April 26, 1906.

Page 93: *Top, Oakland Tribune,* April 20, 1906; *bottom, Berkeley Daily Gazette,* April 26, 1906.

Page 94: Contra Costa Historical Society.

Page 95: *Oakland Tribune,* May 6, 1906.

Chapter Nine

Page 96: Private collection.

Page 97: *Souvenir and Resume of Oakland Relief Work to San Francisco Refugees,* Harris Bishop.

Page 98: *Top, Souvenir and Resume of Oakland Relief Work to San Francisco Refugees,* Harris Bishop; *bottom,* private collection.

Page 99: *Souvenir and Resume of Oakland Relief Work to San Francisco Refugees,* Harris Bishop.

Page 100: *Left, Souvenir and Resume of Oakland Relief Work to San Francisco Refugees,* Harris Bishop; *right,* Oakland History Room, Oakland Public Library.

Page 101: *Oakland Tribune,* May 1, 1906.

Page 102: *Souvenir and Resume of Oakland Relief Work to San Francisco Refugees,* Harris Bishop.

Page 103: Bancroft Library, UC Berkeley, 1905.17500 v.33:177.

Index

Page numbers in *italics* indicate images.

Verges, Germain, *78*
Verges, Maria, *78*
Veteran Reserve, 90
veterans, 89–91
Villa des Roses Restaurant, *78*
Vine Street, *91*, 105
Vollmer, August, *88*, 89–91, *92*, 94
volunteers. *See* relief effort

W
Wagner, Gustave, 11
Wallace, Janette Howard, 54
Waller Street, 27
warehouse district, 74
Warring Street, *13*
Washington School, 17
waterfront, 4, 108
water mains, vii, 14, 30, 32
water supplies for refugees, *53*, 72, 83, 96–97.
   See also sanitation at camps
water tower, *20*

water wagons, *53*
weddings, 87
West Berkeley Bank, 20, *21*
West Berkeley Planing Mill, *3*
Westminster Presbyterian Church, 77
wharf, deepwater, 4, 108
Wharff, William, *90*
Wheeler, Benjamin Ide, 43, *60*, 89, 100, *111*
Whittier (school), 17
Wilson, Frank, 57, 60
Wiseman, Margaret, *91*
Wiseman, William Henry, *90*, *91*
Woodmen Hall, 73

Y
Ye Liberty Playhouse, 107
Yerba Buena Island, 47
YMCA, 73, 74, *76*, 92
York, Berk, 58
Yost, Harold, 1, 4, 9, 15, 79
YWCA, 73